SEE IT. SAY IT. BELIEVE IT. RECEIVE IT.

Manifest *Me*

THE WOMAN'S AWAKENING OF
HER POWER, HER PEACE, AND HER PURPOSE

TESHIA MILTON

SEE IT. SAY IT. BELIEVE IT. RECEIVE IT. Manifest Me The Awakening of Your Power, Your Peace, and Your Purpose © 2026 Teshia Milton.

All Rights Reserved. Published by The Manifestation Experience, LLC

All rights reserved. No part of this book may be reproduced, stored in a retrieval system, or transmitted in any form or by any means—electronic, mechanical, photocopying, recording, scanning, or otherwise—without prior written permission from the publisher, except in the case of brief quotations used in reviews or articles.

This book is a work of nonfiction. While every effort has been made to ensure accuracy, the author assumes no responsibility for any errors or omissions, or for the misuse or misinterpretation of any information contained herein.

The guidance in this book is intended for inspirational and educational purposes only. It is not a substitute for professional mental health, medical, or legal advice. Readers should consult qualified professionals for any such concerns.

Cover Design: Teshia Milton

Interior Design: The Manifestation Experience, LLC

Printed in the United States of America

ISBN: 979-8-9923816-3-4

First Edition: 2026

For permissions, inquiries, or speaking engagements, please contact:

The Manifestation Experience, LLC
Email: info@manifestwithteshia.com
Website: www.manifestwithteshia.com

MANIFEST ME
TABLE OF CONTENTS

Opening Letter — 04

Introduction — 06

Chapter 1 | Foundations of Manifesting Me — 10

Chapter 2 | The Manifest Me Framework — 19

Chapter 3 | The Benefits of Manifesting Me First — 31

Chapter 4 | Attachment Styles & Manifestation Blocks — 53

Chapter 5 | Anxious Attachment — 61

Chapter 6 | Dismissive Avoidant Attachment — 74

Chapter 7 | Fearful Avoidant / Disorganized Attachment — 87

Chapter 8 | Secure Attachment — 101

Chapter 9 | Limerence — 110

Chapter 10 | The Truth — 114

Chapter 11 | Heal, Align, and Become — 118

Chapter 12 | Your Manifest Me Affirmations — 137

Conclusion — The Manifested You — 157

Manifest Me Declaration — 160

Encouragement — 163

Author's Note — 165

My Prayer For You — 167

References and Additional Resources — 169

── LETTER FROM ME TO YOU

Dear Beautiful Woman,

If you are holding this book in your hands, something within you has already shifted. A quiet awareness has stirred, a whisper you could no longer ignore, calling you toward more. Not more responsibility, weight, or expectations, but more of you. This moment marks the beginning of remembering that the life you desire cannot fully bloom until you return to the woman at its center.

This book was written because I understand what it feels like to slowly drift away from yourself while giving everything to everyone else. I know the exhaustion of pouring until you are empty, loving without being met, giving without being held. I know what it is to encourage others while silently wishing someone would notice the heaviness in your own soul. I understand the weight of wearing strength like armor. Not by choice, but because life demanded it. I experienced how lonely it can feel to be needed by many and truly seen by none.

For a long time, I existed as a version of myself shaped by survival. I was capable, dependable, resilient, and strong, yet disconnected from my own identity. There were moments of brilliance, but I lived beneath my potential. I had a voice, but I softened it for the comfort of others. I carried gifts, but I minimized them to avoid disruption. My heart held deep love, yet I gave it freely while accepting far less in return. When I looked in the mirror, the woman staring back was not broken, she was buried.

Everything shifted the moment I realized I could no longer afford to abandon myself. That decision, the choice to return inward, became the foundation of this book.

Manifest Me is not a slogan or a fleeting wave of motivation. It is a reclaiming. It is the journey of rising from a life shaped by trauma, fear, expectations, and survival, into the woman formed by purpose, identity, clarity, and truth.

This book carries the fragments of my own becoming. The tears I shed in silence. The boundaries enforced even when they hurt, and standards I raised out of necessity. The wounds faced with trembling hands, and the parts of myself I finally chose to honor. Writing these words transformed me, and my deepest hope is that reading them transforms you too.

Before you go any further, hear this from the depths of my heart. You are not behind. You are not broken. You are not invisible. You are not too late or too far gone. You are standing in the sacred space between who you have been and who you are being called to become. You are in divine transition; unfolding of a woman rising from her own pain and ashes.

This book is an invitation back to yourself. The mirror you may have avoided, now reflecting the truth of who you are. It is the voice you once silenced, now speaking with clarity and conviction. The place where healing can exhale, where the heart can soften, and where identity can breathe again. My prayer is that these pages walk beside you as a companion. Comforting you when the journey feels heavy, confronting you when you begin to shrink, and reminding you at every step that you were never meant to live small.

The world has known the version of you shaped by survival. You are now stepping into the version shaped by purpose. The woman guided by intuition, grounded in confidence, anchored in wholeness, and aligned with truth. This is your becoming season. The season where you stop running from your reflection and begin embracing the fullness of who you truly are. Where you reclaim your identity and rise into a woman the world has not yet met, but deeply needs.

Thank you for trusting me and allowing these words into the sacred places of your heart. I appreciate you for choosing to pick up this book and, in doing so, choosing yourself. This is more than a journey. This is a homecoming.

Welcome to See It. Say It. Believe It. Receive It.
Manifest Me

With love, truth, and unapologetic purpose,
Teshia

INTRODUCTION

This is Your Becoming Season

INTRODUCTION

THIS IS YOUR BECOMING SEASON

 There comes a moment in a woman's life when she feels the quiet pull of destiny stirring within her spirit, a moment when the inner whisper can no longer be ignored, gently reminding her that there is more meant for her than what she has known.

There is more in you than this. A moment arrives when awareness opens and you realize how many years were spent showing up for everyone else while neglecting yourself, and giving without replenishment. Carrying weight never meant to be held alone, and shrinking for the comfort of others while quietly suffocating under the expectations of the world.

There is a sacred and undeniable moment when a woman truly sees herself. Not the image shaped by survival, obligation, or expectation, but the truth of who she is beneath it all. That moment marks the beginning of her becoming. This is the moment you have reached.

A time comes when the cost of self abandonment can no longer be ignored. Patterns become visible. Sacrifices are acknowledged. Dreams once silenced resurface. Boundaries once overlooked demand attention. It becomes clear that the life built, no matter how full, busy, or productive, has been missing one essential element. Herself.

Manifest Me is the moment you choose to bring her back. It is not a slogan, a trend, or a surge of temporary motivation. It is a summoning of calling forth and reclaiming. The movement from manifesting outcomes to embodying identity. The shift from chasing what you want to becoming the woman who naturally attracts it. The transition from surviving your story to authoring what comes next.

Many women focus on manifesting love, success, stability, peace, provision, or support, without realizing that manifestation is not built on desire but on identity. A life cannot rise beyond the belief you hold about who you are. Abundance cannot flourish in a mindset trained by lack. Healthy love cannot thrive where abandonment is still expected. Peace cannot settle where chaos is given residence.

Nothing you desire can rise higher than the emotional, spiritual, and mental foundation supporting it.

Misalignment mishandles blessings. Fragmentation sabotages opportunity. Insecurity questions what is already deserved. Unhealed wounds filter every gift through fear. This is why Manifest Me begins with you. Not with circumstances, not with relationships, not with outcomes, but with the woman reflected back at you.

When you shift, life responds. When healing takes place, patterns loses its power. When you rise, standards elevate. When alignment is restored, environments adjust. And when you choose yourself, everything connected to you must respond differently. Manifest Me becomes the invitation to stop performing strength and begin living in truth. It is the movement from settling to selecting, from self abandonment to self honoring, from resisting power to walking in it without apology. It is the moment light is no longer dimmed and life is lived in full expression.

This book is not about fixing you, because you are not broken. It is about revealing you; the woman hidden beneath survival, fear, and responsibility. You are stepping into a season where the version of you that played small can no longer exist, where tolerance for disrespect no longer has access, and where fear of your own greatness is left at the threshold of your destiny.

This is your becoming season. A season of returning to identity, softness, power, voice, boundaries, intuition, and worth. This is you rising from spaces that once confined you and aligning with who you were always created to be. A season of manifesting from identity rather than desperation. This is your return to yourself.

And when a woman truly returns to herself, nothing stands in the way of her rise.

CHAPTER 1

Foundations of Manifesting *Me*

CHAPTER 1

FOUNDATIONS OF MANIFESTING ME

 Most women spend their lives trying to fix what exists around them, unaware that real breakthrough begins with transformation within. Schedules are adjusted, relationships shifted, jobs changed, appearances refined, and habits modified, yet fulfillment remains elusive because attention was never given to the condition of the woman beneath the roles she carries.

A woman can pray for peace while carrying inner chaos. She can desire healthy connection while still operating from unresolved abandonment wounds. She can want success while wrestling with beliefs of unworthiness. She longs for stability, yet feeling emotionally unsafe within herself. There is hope for elevation, but quietly fearing she is not enough for the destiny before her. No external shift can last until the inner framework of a woman is restored.

This is the heart of Manifest Me.

Manifesting yourself is not about making life look better. It is about creating alignment within, and the deliberate choice to stop living from wounds and begin living from worth. It is becoming emotionally present with yourself after years of disconnection. Where there is understanding that the next level cannot be entered while holding onto the mindset, fears, and emotional patterns of the last one.

T

Manifesting yourself is the process of releasing identities that no longer serve your growth. The people pleaser. The over-giver. The one who overlooks red flags, tolerates inconsistency, or stays silent to avoid conflict. These versions lose their hold the moment you acknowledge a deeper truth. You deserve more, not because you earned it, but because worth has always been inherent.

Choosing to manifest yourself means facing what was once avoided. Thoughts are refined. Self perception is elevated. Actions begin to reflect the woman you were designed to be. Healing shifts from surface level adjustments to root level restoration.

As this shift takes place, everything connected to you responds. Relationships mirror boundaries. Decisions reflect clarity. Opportunities align with confidence. Peace flows from a healed identity. Lifestyle begins to match the woman you are stepping into.

Manifest Me is not about creating someone new. It is the awakening of who has always been there, buried beneath stress, trauma, expectations, and survival. It is a return to authenticity and wholeness. It is the moment attention moves from fixing the outside to honoring what is forming within.

Here, worth becomes non negotiable. Self abandonment ends. Shrinking loses appeal. Misalignment is no longer chased. Relationships that disturb the spirit are released. Chaos is no longer normalized. In its place stands a woman rooted in peace, clarity, truth, and alignment.

When you manifest yourself, pursuit gives way to attraction. Manifest Me becomes a homecoming, a return to the woman you were always meant to be before fear dimmed your light, before trauma shaped your patterns, and before life taught you to question your value.

Manifest Me is not a destination. It is transformation. It is rebirth into who you truly are.

— YOU ARE THE SOURCE

Every woman carries a depth of power she was never fully taught to recognize. From the outside, it can appear as though life is simply happening to her, when in truth, life is responding through her. She is the center, the emotional and energetic foundation upon which everything in her world is formed.

When a woman rises within herself, her life begins to reflect that elevation. When she disconnects internally, what is connected to her feels the strain. Not because she must carry everything, but because she is the source, the pulse, the inner compass guiding the direction of her life. Relationships, peace, opportunity, boundaries, desire, confidence, and healing all flow from what lives inside her.

A woman can hold immense influence without realizing it. She can shift spaces without understanding why. Her presence can carry spiritual weight even when she doubts herself. Yet without awareness of her own power, she gives it away. She hands her peace to others, waits for validation she already possesses, and hopes for change without recognizing that she is the catalyst.

Life is not waiting on someone else to choose differently. It is not waiting on apologies, promotions, relationships, or permission. It is waiting on you. The aligned, grounded, whole version of you to step forward. You are not merely reflecting what comes toward you. You are setting the tone. You are the one who determines the emotional and energetic climate of your world.

When you believe you are unworthy, life reflects that belief. When you know you deserve more, life stretches to meet that knowing. This is why Manifest Me is a return to your rightful position. It moves you from passenger to driver, from reacting to creating. It reminds you that you are not simply existing within your circumstances, you are shaping them through your thoughts, choices, and internal posture.

When you begin treating yourself as the source, your orientation shifts. Happiness is no longer outsourced to people who were never meant to sustain it. Waiting to be chosen loses its grip because self-selection comes first. The search for external rescuers ends when responsibility for the quality of your life is fully reclaimed.

A woman who recognizes herself as the source becomes deliberate. Her decisions carry weight. Her boundaries reflect self-respect rather than defense. Her standards rise because she understands alignment is her birthright, not something she must earn.

When a woman settles into the truth of who she is, the world responds. Not because circumstances change on their own, but because she does. As identity elevates, life adjusts to match it. Her voice is received with respect. Her connections begin mirroring honor. As peace is protected, surroundings reorganize to support it. As worth is embodied, opportunities respond in kind.

Living as the source ends the habit of chasing what already exists within you. It dissolves the need to beg for what was always yours. Manifest Me restores you to the center of your own life, the place that was never meant to be abandoned. It reveals that identity fuels manifestation, boundaries protect elevation, and self-belief is the ground where the next level takes root.

You are not a byproduct of your circumstances. You are the architect of your reality. The moment this truth is embraced, everything in your life begins to shift in your favor.

—— IDENTITY: THE ROOT OF YOUR REALITY

Everything in your life flows from the identity you carry at your core. Not the version you present to the world or the role you perform in public, but the quiet belief system beneath it all. That inner truth shapes your choices, your connections, your limits, and the dreams you permit yourself to pursue. It governs how you show up, what you accept, and what you unknowingly draw toward you.

A woman can long for a better life with sincerity. She can pray for it, work toward it, and grieve over the distance between where she is and where she wants to be. Yet when her sense of self is rooted in survival, her decisions will continue reinforcing that foundation. Desires and behaviors fall out of alignment. Patterns contradict intentions. Outcomes echo the inner world.

Identity is the unseen script beneath habits, fears, and hopes. It is the inner narrator defining who you are when no one is watching. When that voice is wounded, life reflects the wound. When it is afraid, life contracts, and when it remains unhealed, cycles repeat.

A woman who believes she is unlovable will often disrupt genuine affection, not out of desire to lose it, but because her inner capacity has not yet learned how to hold it. When love feels conditional, she overextends herself, giving more than is sustainable in an attempt to earn what was never meant to be earned. When she views herself as second best, she enters spaces with gratitude instead of belonging. Identity shapes reality far more powerfully than circumstance ever could.

This is why Manifest Me begins with reprogramming the inner narrative. It is the conscious choice to quiet the voice that insists you are lacking and replace it with truth. It is moving from resignation to expectancy, from anticipation of loss to openness to alignment, and from fear based conclusions to grounded knowing.

This work is not wishful thinking. It is a reconstruction. It is the intentional rewriting of the emotional blueprint that has guided your life until now.

It requires questioning inherited beliefs, challenging learned fears, and releasing narratives formed during seasons of survival. It is the decision to live from wholeness rather than fragments.

The truth is simple and profound. Transformation does not begin with circumstance. It begins with self perception. The woman you believe yourself to be determines the life you allow yourself to live. When identity shifts, reality begins rearranging itself in response.

Your life follows your identity, and identity shapes experience. When you elevate what you believe about who you are, everything around you must rise to meet that truth.

— BREAKING LIMITING BELIEFS

Limiting beliefs are quiet prisons learned over time. Spaces we inhabit without ever questioning how we arrived there. They are invisible restraints around a woman's potential, tightening whenever she attempts to stretch into what is next. These false narratives repeat themselves so steadily that they begin to feel like truth.

They operate beneath awareness, influencing decisions, shaping connections, informing confidence, and narrowing dreams.

A woman may long for abundance with her whole being, but if she carries the belief that abundance is unsafe, she will disrupt it the moment it arrives. She may even ache for love, but if her inner world expects abandonment or betrayal, she will choose familiarity over health, and repeat old wounds instead of receiving honor. She may envision success, but if she was taught that visibility is dangerous or growth is selfish, she will dim herself to avoid surpassing others.

Limiting beliefs rarely announce themselves. They speak softly, and do not arrive dramatically. They linger in the background, shaping behavior gradually until they feel indistinguishable from identity itself.

Most of these beliefs were never yours by origin. They were absorbed through early environments where affection was inconsistent or conditional. They formed through painful connections that distorted self worth. These beliefs were reinforced by cultural messages urging silence, shrinking, or settling, and they took root in spaces where survival was prioritized over expression.

And over time, what began as protection became limitation, quietly defining what felt possible long before you ever questioned whether it was true.

Because those beliefs took root early, they begin to feel familiar, almost comforting. Familiarity is mistaken for truth. Comfort is mistaken for safety. Without realizing it, a woman learns to live beneath her own capacity, shrinking into an identity she never consciously chose. These patterns settle quietly, shaping how she loves, how she shows up, and what she believes she deserves.

Manifest Me interrupts that cycle.

It invites you to look beneath behavior and examine the beliefs driving it. It asks you to question every so-called truth you absorbed but never selected. Manifest Me confronts the narratives that have been directing your life on autopilot. The ones that said you were too much or not enough. Too emotional. Too needy. Too ambitious. Too complicated. Too broken. Too late. It challenges the scripts that whisper limits: you can have some, but not more; you can be loved, but not fully; you can rise, but not beyond others; you can feel confident, but not powerful; you can speak, but not boldly.

Then it replaces them with truth, one that resonates at a higher frequency and aligns with who you were always meant to be.

Breaking limiting beliefs is not merely mindset work. It is liberation of identity, and the realization that you have been living within an emotional inheritance you never agreed to accept. It is the moment patterns are seen clearly, not as measures of worth, but as echoes of wounds. The decision to stop letting fear instruct you, pain direct you, or the past define what is possible.

When a limiting belief breaks, the atmosphere of life shifts. What once felt impossible begins to feel accessible. Doors assumed to be locked begin to open. Opportunities once avoided now feel aligned. Love that feels unsafe becomes receivable. Confidence that was performed becomes embodied. This is the power of belief transformation. It rewrites the inner script so the outer world can rise to meet the woman you are becoming.

Most women do not fall short because effort is missing. They fall short because identity has been confined. When a limiting belief is broken, every cycle connected to it begins to dissolve. Generational patterns loosen. Emotional restraints release. The ceiling that once hovered over destiny lifts.

Manifest Me invites you into this truth. You are not defined by the lies that shaped your past. You are empowered by the truth that is shaping your future. Releasing limiting beliefs is not only mental work. It is spiritual reconstruction. It is emotional rebirth and identity elevation. The focus shifts from adjusting to circumstances to shaping life from the inside out. As false beliefs fall away, the life designed for you, the one that has been calling to your spirit for years, becomes accessible. Becoming the woman you are meant to be requires releasing the lies spoken over the girl you once were.

This is liberation. This is awakening. This is where the next level begins.

CHAPTER 2

The Manifest Me Framework

CHAPTER 2

THE MANIFEST ME FRAMEWORK

 Manifest Me is not a fleeting spark of inspiration. It is a metamorphosis. A shedding of old skin, a dissolving of former identities, and a release of emotional residue carried for far too long. This transformation unfolds through four sacred movements, each one gently removing what no longer belongs so the truth of who you are can emerge. Seeing, speaking, believing, and receiving are not assignments to complete. They are spiritual actions. Together, they work in harmony to restore a woman from the inside out. They reshape the inner world, realign identity, and rebuild the foundation from which everything else flows. These movements form the inner architecture of transformation. They are the blueprint for your rising.

These movements shift far more than habits. They transform the inner world. They reshape how you see yourself, how you speak inwardly, how you interpret experience, and how fully you inhabit your identity. As you move through them, clarity emerges that manifestation begins long before anything appears in physical form. It starts in thought, emotion, belief, and posture. It begins within you.

—— SEE IT: THE COURAGE TO FACE YOU

Seeing is the first and most powerful movement because nothing in your life can change until you are willing to acknowledge what is truly happening within you. True seeing is not casual awareness. It is a divine unveiling, and sacred moment when the fog lifts and you stop running from the reality of your inner world. It begins the instant you allow yourself to witness the parts of you that were hidden, minimized, or ignored, the parts you feared would undo you if faced.

Seeing requires courage and invites you to look at who you have been without condemnation. It asks you to admit that some choices were shaped by fear instead of faith, silence instead of truth, and survival instead of identity. It brings you face to face with the version of you who learned to perform strength because softness never felt safe, and calls you to acknowledge desires buried beneath responsibility and pain, desires you convinced yourself no longer mattered.

Seeing also asks you to accept a difficult truth. Some patterns were never consciously chosen. They were inherited, conditioned, or formed in environments where your needs went unseen. And yet, within that honesty, seeing becomes deeply freeing.

Seeing is not only about acknowledging where you have been. It is also about vision and learning to see yourself as God designed you to be, whole, confident, restored, and aligned with purpose. It is allowing your imagination to be redeemed, to picture the woman God has always seen even when you could not. This kind of seeing bridges honesty with hope, truth with promise, and reality with destiny.

This is the moment clarity arrives and you begin to understand why you tolerated what hurt you. Not from weakness, but from a lack of emotional safety. You see why certain cycles repeated, not because you were incapable, but because they felt familiar. You recognize why you accepted less than you deserved, not because you did not know your worth, but because you feared that claiming it would cost you connection. You finally understand why self doubt lingered even when others could clearly recognize your brilliance.

This awareness breaks something open within you. It restores truth, and reminds you that you are valuable, deserving, and worthy of the fullness life has to offer, exactly as God intended.

Seeing is the gateway to liberation. It is the threshold you must cross before cycles can be broken, old narratives dismantled, and a new identity embraced. When you finally see yourself clearly, something irreversible awakens within you. Patterns that no longer align lose their grip. Loyalty to versions you have outgrown quietly dissolves. Seeing does not bring shame. It brings freedom.

Seeing is the moment truth is chosen over comfort, alignment replaces avoidance, and identity replaces illusion. You see the woman you are becoming, rather than the woman you have been. Awareness rises the instant you stop settling for what wounds were willing to accept and begin honoring the deeper knowing that you were created for more.

Seeing is also learning to view yourself through God's eyes. Not through the lens of failure, fear, or past mistakes, but through divine intention and purpose. It is allowing His perspective to redefine your worth, your potential, and your future. When you see yourself as God sees you, you stop measuring life by limitation and begin aligning with calling.

Transformation begins here because clarity reveals what is required to rise. Change does not start with action. It starts with awareness. When you see yourself with honesty, grace, and divine vision, you step into the first true moment of becoming. From that point forward, nothing can remain unchanged.

— SAY IT: THE LANGUAGE OF IDENTITY

Speaking is the second sacred movement of the Manifest Me transformation, and it carries far more power than most women have been taught to recognize. Your voice is not merely sound. It is a spiritual instrument that carries authority, intention, energy, and power. The words you release over your life, whether spoken aloud or whispered internally, becomes the blueprint from which your reality is formed.

Every woman speaks from identity. When identity is rooted in insecurity, language reflects fear, doubt, and unworthiness. Words rise from old wounds rather than present truth. Narratives inherited before choice was possible continue to repeat themselves. She speaks in ways that reduce her presence because she learned that shrinking once felt safer, more acceptable, or more lovable.

But when healing begins, true healing, language changes. Speech no longer originates from pain but from emergence. Words align with destiny rather than history. Voice steadies. Expression strengthens. Language begins to honor worth instead of undermining it. What she speaks starts to come from where she is going, not from what once hurt her.

Speaking is not surface positivity or empty affirmations. It is intentional declarations. It is choosing to let language reflect identity in formation rather than identity left behind. Words hold power to shape emotion, direct focus, influence decision making, and determine movement. What you speak consistently, you eventually live.

A woman who reclaims her voice does not speak simply to be heard. She speaks to become. She uses language to bring alignment between her inner world and her vision. She reinforces truth until it feels natural, anchors herself in worth, and interrupts the internal scripts that once kept her diminished. Through speaking, she reminds her spirit of who she is and what she is worthy of.

In this movement, voice becomes activation. What was once silent finds expression. What was once hidden gains clarity. And with every aligned word spoken, identity strengthens and reality begins to follow.

And as your language shifts, something miraculous begins to unfold. Your reality starts responding. You learn that the way you speak about yourself reshapes how you treat yourself. You notice the way you speak about your future influences how you pursue it, and the way you speak about your life changes how others experience you.

Speaking becomes the bridge between seeing and believing. It is the point where your voice stops undermining you and starts constructing you.

When a woman speaks from her sense of being, her words become the first visible evidence of who she is becoming. The more her language aligns with truth, the more life rearranges itself to honor the woman she is rising into.

There is also a deeper, spiritual dimension to speaking. Scripture reminds us that life and death are in the power of the tongue, and that God Himself spoke creation into existence. Light appeared because He said it. Order emerged because He declared it. What God speaks carries creative authority, and when a woman aligns her voice with what God has already spoken over her life, she begins to partner with that same divine principle.

Speaking in alignment with God is not forcing outcomes. It is agreement. It is choosing to echo heaven rather than repeat history. When you speak what God says about you, chosen, worthy, loved, called, whole, you activate truth over every lie that once governed your inner world. Your words stop rehearsing fear and begin reinforcing promise.

This kind of speaking requires faith. It means declaring what God revealed even when circumstances have not yet caught up. It means calling yourself healed while healing is still unfolding, confident while confidence is still forming, and purposeful while purpose is still being revealed. Faith filled words do not deny reality. They shape it.

When your voice aligns with God's Word, speaking becomes creation rather than commentary. You are no longer describing what you see. You are declaring what God has said. This the power of speaking is not just expression, it is an agreement with God. It is the moment your mouth becomes an instrument of transformation, and your life begins to follow the sound of your own aligned voice.

——BELIEVE IT: THE INNER AGREEMENT

Believing is the third and most intimate movement of the Manifest Me transformation. This is where the work shifts from what you can see and speak to what you are willing to hold within. Belief is not a passing thought. It is a state of being. It is not hope or wishing. It is a deep, embodied knowing.

A woman can visualize a new life and speak new words, yet if she quietly believes she is unworthy, unsafe, or incapable of sustaining that life, she will resist what she desires without realizing it. This is because belief sets the emotional climate of selfhood. It is the inner atmosphere that determines whether blessings can land, take root, and remain.

Belief lives in the body. It resides in the nervous system, emotional reactions, triggers, and expectations. The body remembers what it survived, what it feared, and what it learned to anticipate. So even when the mind declares readiness, the body may still signal danger. Believing requires teaching the body and spirit a new truth, one grounded in safety rather than survival.

A woman cannot fully receive love she does not believe she deserves. She cannot sustain abundance if she expects it to vanish. She cannot rise into power if she fears isolation. Confidence cannot stabilize when the voice within has been conditioned to distrust itself. Belief determines capacity.

Believing is not the narrative shared publicly. It is the conversation held internally when no one else is listening. It requires an internal shift so complete that former narratives lose their authority. It involves emotional rewiring, releasing loyalty to fear, and letting go of expectations formed in survival seasons. The beliefs that once protected the girl must be replaced by beliefs that elevate the woman.

This movement is a quiet but powerful handoff. Belief becomes the moment the woman you are becoming speaks gently to the girl you once were and says, "I've got it from here."

Believing means you stop viewing your future through the lens of your past. Old wounds are no longer used as present filters. Instead, you give yourself permission to imagine, expect, and prepare for a life that looks nothing like what hurts you. Belief becomes the bridge between who you were and who you are becoming.

Believing also means you begin expecting good without bracing for loss. The habit of preparing for disappointment loosens its grip, and space is made to receive stability, joy, and consistency. Peace is no longer treated as temporary. It becomes a place you are worthy of inhabiting daily.

Believing teaches your spirit that abundance is not unstable, but aligned. Overflow is understood as inheritance rather than accident. The nervous system is retrained to feel safe with love, support, and visibility. Flinching at goodness fades. Questioning blessings quiets. You settle into the truth that what is arriving belongs to you.

Belief is not a single moment. It is a quiet, ongoing agreement with transformation. It is the daily decision to see yourself through the eyes of your heavenly father, rather than through the wounds you survived. It is the internal posture that says to God, "I am ready to receive what You have prepared for me." As belief deepens, behavior begins to align. Chasing ends because worth is known. Breadcrumbs lose appeal because abundance is expected.

Believing is the shift from hoping to knowing. It is standing firm even when circumstances have not yet caught up. It is allowing the future to feel more real than the past. Belief becomes the quiet doorway between becoming and breakthrough. And when a woman truly believes, everything about her changes. Energy steadies. Decisions sharpen. Boundaries strengthen. Standards rise. Intuition clarifies. The heart becomes grounded, and belief becomes the birthplace of manifestation.

Believing is also an act of faith. It is trusting what God has spoken even when evidence is still forming. It is choosing confidence in divine promise over attachment to visible proof. Faith allows you to walk forward without needing reassurance at every step.

Faith filled belief does not deny reality. It anchors you beyond it. It holds space for what is unfolding while remaining rooted in what is true. When belief is anchored in faith, fear loses its authority. Doubt no longer dictates direction and the heart rests in expectancy rather than anxiety.

When you learn to believe differently, your life begins to unfold differently. Belief is not merely a part of transformation. It is transformation. It is the sacred agreement with the life you were always created to live.

—— RECEIVE IT: THE EMBODIMENT OF BECOMING

Receiving is the final movement of Manifest Me, and it is the most transformative because it requires you to become the woman you have been praying, healing, and preparing for. The shift from inner awakening to outer embodiment.

Receiving is often misunderstood. Many think receiving means waiting for blessings to arrive, as if manifestation is passive. As if it is something that happens to you. But receiving is not passive. It is not idle. It is not standing still with open hands and old habits. Receiving is active and intentional. The courageous decision to walk in the reality of who you are before the evidence appears. Receiving is the practice of living as if the doors are already open, even when you are still standing in the hallway.

Receiving requires you to embody the woman you have been creating inside of you. It requires you to make decisions that honor your next level rather than accommodate your past. It demands that your standards reflect your worth instead of your wound, and It asks you to rise into the version of yourself that your future depends on.

A woman who is ready to receive does not wait for permission. There is no such thing as perfect timing. No need to wait for validation or applause. She moves and chooses differently. She thinks differently. She carries herself with the quiet confidence of a woman who understands that what is hers is already on its way.

Receiving asks you to behave like the woman who already has what she desires.

It means you begin walking with the confidence of a woman who is worthy of love, respect, abundance, stability, and peace; because she is. You carry yourself differently when you finally recognize your own value. You stop shrinking and apologizing for taking up space that was always yours to claim.

It means you begin making decisions from faith rather than fear, because alignment has become your new standard. You no longer choose from insecurity or desperation, instead, you choose from clarity.

You begin moving through life with the energy of someone who expects good things. You live with an open heart, a steady mind, and a spirit that knows goodness is your portion.

Receiving requires emotional courage. It invites you to let go of the version of yourself who tolerated too much, and release the narratives that kept you in cycles of lack. Your goal is to experience success without waiting for something to go wrong, and choose joy without thinking you need to earn it.

Receiving teaches you that worthiness is not something you chase. It is something you stand in. The more you receive internally, the more your external world adjusts to match your identity. Opportunities begin to present themselves more clearly. Relationships begin to align with your standards. Doors open that once felt locked. Circumstances shift in ways that feel both miraculous and inevitable. Receiving is the moment your entire life begins to reorganize itself around your new self-perception.

It is the moment your posture says, "I am ready," even if your past once said otherwise. Your actions finally match your prayers. The moment your energy aligns with your elevation, you stop sabotaging what you once begged for. It is the moment you choose to live as though the breakthrough has already happened, because internally, it has.

Receiving is not about getting something. Receiving is about becoming who you were created to be. It is becoming the woman who naturally attracts love because she is aligned with love. The woman who draws abundance because her identity no longer resists the overflow she deserves. She commands respect because she holds a deep reservoir of self-respect within. It is being the woman who walks in peace because chaos is no longer her home. The woman who can hold blessings without fear because she has been rebuilt strong enough to sustain them.

Receiving is the final movement of transformation because embodiment is the highest expression of being. You cannot truly step into the next level until you are willing to live from that level. Receiving is the quiet boldness of stepping forward without hesitation. It is the emotional readiness to allow blessings to remain rather than slip through your fingers. Spiritual alignment that tells your God, "I am prepared."

CHAPTER 3

The Benefits of Manifesting Me First

CHAPTER 3

THE BENEFITS OF MANIFESTING ME FIRST

 There comes a moment in a woman's life when she realizes that the version of herself she has been living as is only a fraction of who she truly is. A moment when she feels the quiet whisper of her own identity calling her higher. She can no longer deny the truth that she has spent years dimming: I am the foundation. I am the source. I am the center of my change.

Manifesting yourself first is not an act of selfishness. It is an act of sacred responsibility. It is the acknowledgment that everything in your life flows through you: your energy, your beliefs, your boundaries, and your standards. When you elevate the woman, you elevate the world she touches. When you heal the woman, you heal the spaces she occupies.

A woman who chooses herself becomes a force to be reckoned with. She becomes clear and grounded. Not because she is trying to prove anything to anyone, but because she finally understands that her life expands in direct proportion to how deeply she honors herself.

When you manifest yourself first, your relationships transform. Not because other people change, but because you do. The woman who once tolerated inconsistency suddenly realizes that peace is her baseline.

Where emotional breadcrumbs were enough, she now begins to expect full nourishment. The woman who once begged to be chosen learns to choose herself without hesitation. The one who feared being alone, begins to recognize the privilege, power, and peace found in her own company. Her internal shift becomes her liberation, and everything around her begins to adjust.

People who cannot match her healed identity naturally fall away. Those who thrive in chaos lose access to her. Individuals who benefited from her silence become uncomfortable in her voice. And those who once drained her spirit, slowly lose their place in her story. Not because she is bitter, but because she is better.

Manifesting yourself first creates a new relational blueprint. It is one built not on fear, survival, or abandonment wounds, but on mutual respect, emotional safety, and authentic connections.

When a woman rises, she inevitably sheds what kept her low. Her relationships begin to mirror her new emotional frequency. They are higher and purer. Connections deepen with those who honor her growth. Conversations shift toward purpose. Her boundaries strengthen effortlessly, and peace becomes her new home.

—— YOUR EMOTIONAL WORLD ELEVATES WITH YOU

When a woman chooses herself, she makes her emotional world undergo a radical transformation. It is not a surface level shift, a motivational moment, or a new burst of inspiration. It is an internal reorientation. Something within her arranges itself quietly. She becomes different on the inside long before her life reflects it. Where she once reacted from fear, she now pauses, breathes, and responds from wisdom. Spiraling into worry is not a part of her expression. She now grounds herself in truth. Questioning her worth is not a thought, but she now stands in it with authority that cannot be shaken. Her emotional body begins to learn a new language. The language of stability, strength, and self-trust.

The woman she used to be was shaped by survival. Her instincts were conditioned by instability, disappointment, and by unpredictable environments she learned to navigate long before she even understood herself.

She became who she needed to be to endure everyday life. The woman she is choosing is shaped by intention. She is shaped by her willingness to release what was and embrace what is to be. Her inner world shifts from chaotic to clear, from reactive to grounded, from fearful to discerning, and from anxious to anchored. Although the transformation is not loud, its effects are profound. It does not happen overnight, but it unfolds in every choice, every boundary, and every moment she decides to see herself differently.

Manifesting Me is not about controlling emotions or pretending to be unaffected by life. It is about evolving your emotional landscape so you can navigate life with clarity instead of chaos. It is learning how to hold yourself with compassion when old patterns try to resurface. A new way to speak to yourself with truth when insecurity tries to whisper lies. Mastering how to regulate your mind, your breath, and your reactions with grace rather than judgment. Emotional mastery is not perfection, but it is presence, gentle commitment to meet yourself where you are and guide yourself toward where you are.

The woman who manifests herself first becomes emotionally safe within her own mind. She is no longer her own battlefield. She becomes her own place of refuge, her own anchor, her own steady ground. Emotional safety becomes the soil where confidence grows without force. Security becomes the root that allows peace to flourish. Self-trust becomes the foundation upon which her decisions are built. She no longer searches for reassurance the way she once did, because she is now the reassurance she used to seek.

And as her emotional world evolves, the world around her must evolve as well. A woman who is grounded internally becomes unshakeable externally. When she is anchored, her truth cannot be easily manipulated, diminished, or thrown off course. A woman who feels safe with herself becomes magnetic; drawing in people, opportunities, and experiences that reflect the stability she has cultivated. The transformation begins within, but its impact radiates into every area of her life. This is the power of choosing yourself, and the heart of Manifesting Me.

—— YOUR DECISIONS TRANSFORM AS YOUR IDENTITY EXPANDS

When a woman truly knows who she is, everything she chooses begins to reflect that identity. Decisions that once felt confusing suddenly become simple. Boundaries that once felt hard to set, transform into non-negotiables. Opportunities that seemed intimidating, now appear as invitations waiting to be accepted. Her life begins to flow differently because her self-awareness has shifted the standards she lives by.

She stops negotiating her value because she has outgrown the version of herself who accepted discounts on her worth. She no longer chooses from old wounds, because she has intentionally healed the parts of herself that once sought validation through pain. Allowing temporary emotions to sabotage long-term blessings are of the past, because her future has become more important than her fears. Her transformation becomes evident in what and who she no longer entertains.

Manifesting yourself first clarifies your vision. It sharpens your instincts, amplifies your discernment, and elevates your choices. You start showing up in the world differently because your identity is no longer blurred by insecurity, people-pleasing, or self-doubt.

You begin choosing from security instead of insecurity, from clarity instead of confusion, from alignment instead of desperation, and from self-respect instead of self-abandonment. Every decision you make becomes a declaration of who you are. It says loudly and boldly: I know exactly who I am, and I refuse to choose anything that betrays that truth.

—— YOUR RISE CREATES A RISE IN EVERYTHING CONNECTED TO YOU

Long before the external shifts occur, something inside her begins to rise. And when she rises, the temperature of her entire environment rises with her. The atmosphere around her adjusts to her new internal climate. Her relationships strengthen because she no longer accepts connections that drain or diminish her. Her opportunities expand because she begins to believe she is worthy of what once intimidated her. Her standards sharpen because she finally understands that what she allows is a reflection of what she believes she deserves. Her energy grows lighter as she releases what once weighed her spirit down. Her life begins to align. Not with who she used to be, but with the woman she is. Rising does not require noise or announcement. It is not performative. It is quiet, yet deeply spiritual.

Rising is the moment a woman returns to herself. It is when she stops ignoring her needs to maintain connections that do not honor her. It is when she refuses to silence her voice just to be accepted or avoid conflict.

It is when she no longer apologizes for her worth or shrinks herself for the comfort of others. Rising is when she makes peace with the truth that her boundaries are not walls. They are declarations of self-respect. She finally stops sacrificing her identity to uphold a peace that was never real in the first place. Rising is reclaiming the pieces of herself she left behind during survival.

It is remembering who she was before heartbreak trained her to hide, disappointments taught her to settle, and life convinced her to question her value. Rising is realignment with her truth after years of living beneath it. It is a spiritual rebirth into the fullness of who she truly is: healed, whole, grounded, and unapologetically herself.

And when she rises, everything connected to her rises as well. Her relationships shift because she no longer entertains anything that disrupts her peace. Her decisions elevate from clarity, not confusion. Her confidence expands. She no longer doubts her worthiness.

Her emotional world stabilizes because she has learned how to hold herself, soothe herself, and lead herself with grace. Her vision sharpens because she finally sees beyond fear and limitation. Manifesting yourself first is not just a step in your becoming; it is the becoming. It is the foundational transformation that shifts your life from autopilot to moving with intentions.

Rising reshapes not only what she does but who she is. It changes the way she speaks over herself. It is the moment she stops waiting for permission to exist fully and begin embodying the woman she was created to be.

Because when a woman rises, she does not just elevate her life, she elevates her world. She becomes a catalyst for transformation. A reflection of what is possible when identity is reclaimed and self-worth becomes the foundation. Her rise becomes a vibration that touches every corner of her life and everyone connected to her. And that rise marks the beginning of a new reality. One she is no longer afraid to claim, embody, or receive.

— SHE NO LONGER ALLOWS FEAR TO LEAD

When fear is not leading her path, the emotional patterns that once controlled her steps now lose their authority. Fear may still whisper, but it no longer commands her. Anxiety may continue to knock on the door of her emotions, but it's not powerful enough to guide her. Fear is not the narrator of her life or anxiety the architect of her decisions. Instead of reacting from old wounds, she responds from new wisdom. Without fear, she rests in the truth of who she is.

Where she once braced for the worst, she now expects greatness. Her mind begins to shift from protecting herself to preparing herself. She believes in her ability to navigate life with stability rather than being swept away by internal storms. Where she once prepared for rejection, she now understands her worthiness without question. She no longer interprets silence as abandonment or distance as disapproval. She is grounded in the truth that she is deserving of what is meant for her.

She stops assuming something will go wrong, and preparing for betrayal as a default response. She puts an end to rehearsing worst-case scenarios as a form of false protection. She ceases from shrinking to stay safe, realizing that playing small never protected her; it only confined her. As her emotional world evolves, she releases the habits that once kept her in survival mode. She no longer uses fear as a compass, anxiety as a routine, or doubt as her internal language.

A healed emotional world shifts her internal posture from defense to acceptance. She no longer walks through life bracing for impact, but walks free. Her energy, once tense and guarded, becomes open and receptive. She begins moving toward her destiny instead of away from her fears. Her inner world becomes a place of trust. And as she evolves internally, her external world begins to mirror the woman on the inside. She is wise, worthy, and whole.

— SHE TRUSTS THE WISDOM INSIDE HER MORE THAN THE OPINIONS AROUND HER

A woman who is emotionally healthy becomes deeply intuitive. Not because she suddenly knows everything, but because she finally trusts herself enough to listen. Intuition has always been present within her; whispering, nudging, and gently guiding. But emotional instability once made those whispers difficult to discern. Fear distorted those intuitions, while anxiety confused them, and trauma absolutely muted them. But as she heals, the noise fades, and her inner voice becomes clearer, steadier, and unmistakably sacred. She begins to recognize that her intuition is not mysterious or accidental. It is the Holy Spirit speaking to her from within, leading her into truth. What once felt like guesswork now feels like divine direction.

She begins to trust her instincts in ways she never could before because she recognizes them as spiritual signals, and not emotional reactions. The subtle cues in her body that once felt overwhelming now, feels like God-given guidance. She trusts her boundaries, not merely as self-protection, but as spiritual stewardship over her peace.

With discernment, she knows the difference between the familiar patterns of her past and the aligned paths ordained for her future. She trusts her emotional signals. Understanding that discomfort is often the Holy Spirit's way of alerting her, not condemning her. She trusts her internal red flags, even when others dismiss them. Because she knows God whispers warnings long before danger becomes visible. And she trusts her inner peace, recognizing that peace is one of God's loudest confirmations, and anything requiring her to sacrifice that peace is not from Him.

She no longer relies on external validation to make decisions because she knows that divine instruction does not require human approval. The opinions of others no longer outweigh the wisdom God is revealing within her. There is no need for her to consult fear before moving forward. Although fear was taught by her past, she understands her faith is anchored in her future. She recognizes that shrinking herself to keep false peace, never created harmony. It only created silent resentment and spiritual suffocation. She no longer doubts her intuition simply because others disagree. She understands that her journey is God-guided, and her destiny is not a committee assignment.

Her emotional health gives her a steady inner voice. A voice that once whispered, but now speaks with divine affirmation. She honors that voice because it has proven itself trustworthy. It carries the tone of the Holy Spirit: gentle yet firm, soft yet certain, quiet yet undeniable. That inner voice guides her through decisions that once overwhelmed her, through relationships that once unsettled her, and through opportunities she once doubted she deserved. It anchors her when the world becomes noisy. Her voice leads her toward paths aligned with God's assignment for her life. Her intuition becomes her light, and her spiritual GPS. Not because it comes from her alone, but because it is God working through her, and speaking within her.

The more she honors her intuition, the more powerful it becomes. Her emotional world no longer feels like a battlefield. It becomes a sanctuary where wisdom, peace, clarity, and truth lives. Her self-awareness kicks in high gear. Her decisions are no longer a load to carry. Her path becomes clearer and is guided from within. This is the awakening that happens when she chooses to manifest herself first.

— THIS EMOTIONAL STABILITY SHOWS UP IN EVERY AREA OF HER LIFE

There is an undeniable shift in the presence of a grounded woman that people feel before she ever opens her mouth. You can sense her clarity before she speaks. A stillness that shows she is not led by confusion or insecurity. You can feel a calmness that radiates from her spirit and reassures everyone around her. You can see her wisdom in how she carries herself.

Not loudly, or performatively, but with quiet authority and bold confidence. Her emotional health becomes visible long before she tells her story. It shows up in the posture of her heart, the steadiness of her decisions, and the softness of her strength.

Her emotional health reveals itself in how she communicates directly, respectfully, and without fear. It shows in how she thinks clearly. Because her mind is not a battleground of anxieties, but a place where discernment lives. It is evident how she leads confidently and compassionately, and always with boundaries that protects her calling. She loves openly and steadily, yet never at the expense of losing herself. She confronts challenges with strategy instead of spiraling. She knows how to pray instead of panic. It's clear she advocates for herself with dignity, because she knows who she is and who she belongs to. Responding to life with discernment is a norm, because external chaos does not dictate her internal atmosphere.

She becomes a woman who no longer feels attacked by life, but prepared for it. Not because challenges disappear, but because she is fortified on the inside. She is spiritually grounded, emotionally mature, mentally steady, and aligned with God's guidance. Life no longer surprises her in ways that unravels her. Her way of life is to meet every season with a readiness formed through healing and expectation. She becomes the kind of woman who can hold joy without fear, responsibility without being overwhelmed, and relationships without self-abandonment.

Emotional health does for her spirit what strength does for her body. It fortifies her, centers her, and supports her ability to rise. It becomes her internal armor, and not hard or rigid, but stable and secure. It allows her to move through life with a grace that cannot be shaken. She has a confidence that does not need to be announced. This mindset becomes the foundation for a new kind of living, because she makes wiser decisions.

She hears God more clearly, which helps her attract healthier relationships. She trusts herself more deeply which causes her to rise without hesitation and walk in her purpose without apology. The outcome of this mindset is a woman fully equipped and walks in who God created her to be. Her life begins to reflect the stability of her spirit. Opportunities match her capacity, because it is increased. Doors begin to swing open for her. Her environment shifts to accommodate her elevation, and her destiny becomes clearer because she is finally steady enough to receive it. A grounded woman's entire world is elevated.

—— HER EMOTIONS BECOME HER ANCHOR; NOT HER BATTLEFIELD

Before healing, her emotions felt like storms she had to survive. Tension lived in her chest. Fear lived in her mind. Overthinking lived in her decisions, and self-doubt lived in her identity. Every feeling felt heavy, unpredictable, and overwhelming. As if her internal world was constantly shifting beneath her feet. She moved through life bracing for emotional impact. Unsure of when the next wave of fear or anxiety would rise. Her emotions felt bigger, louder, and stronger than her ability to control them.

But when emotional health becomes her foundation, her internal world transforms into peaceful territory. She no longer walks through life afraid of what she feels. Her emotions are not like waves crashing over her. They feel like tides she can navigate with wisdom and grace. What once drowned her, now simply informs her. She learns to breathe through her feelings instead of collapsing under them. Her sensitivity no longer feels like a weakness. She recognizes it as a divine way of sensing truth and warning.

She doesn't have a need to avoid her emotions, because they no longer intimidate her. Instead, she honors them as a message sent to reveal what needs healing, what needs shifting, and what needs releasing. She no longer rejects her needs or criticizes herself for having them. She nurtures those needs with compassion, understanding that emotional awareness is not fragility. It is strength.

Her emotional world stops being the place she runs from and becomes the place she returns to. It becomes a home she can trust, a sanctuary she can rest in, and a landscape she can navigate with clarity. What was once chaos becomes clarity. Fear becomes understanding, and instability becomes peace. When a woman heals emotionally, her inner world becomes her anchor, not her adversary.

—— EMOTIONAL HEALTH BECOMES HER SUPERPOWER

A woman who is emotionally healthy loves better, leads better, chooses better, communicates better, partners better, parents better, works better, heals better, receives better, and ultimately lives better. She becomes a woman operating from wholeness instead of wounds. Her ability to love improves not because people around her suddenly change, but because she has learned to love herself well. And self-love becomes the standard for how she gives and receives affection. She leads better because she is no longer leading from fear or burnout, but from overflow, discernment, and inner stability. Her choices transform because she no longer chooses from desperation, trauma patterns, or emotional voids. She knows she has choices, so she chooses from alignment, purpose, and a grounded sense of worth. Every part of her life becomes a reflection of this inner shift.

Not because life becomes easier, but because she becomes stronger. Healing does not remove the weight of life. It increases her capacity to carry it with grace. She no longer breaks under pressure because she has learned to breathe through it, pray through it, and discern her way through it. Emotional strength is not loud or aggressive. It is quiet resilience. The kind that allows her to stand firm even when everything around her is shifting. She develops the ability to pause before reacting. To stop and process before speaking. To discern before deciding. Her emotions stop dragging her into chaos and start guiding her toward clarity. She becomes a woman who is not strengthened by avoidance but by awareness.

Emotional stability does not remove challenges. It equips her to rise above them. She is no longer blindsided by difficulty because she has developed the inner resources to navigate it.

Instead of spiraling into panic or shutting down emotionally, she approaches challenges with calm problem-solving, spiritual insight, and mental clarity. She recognizes that adversity is not a sign of failure but an opportunity for growth and elevation. She stops interpreting challenges as personal attacks and starts seeing them as invitations to strengthen her boundaries, deepen her faith, and reinforce her alignment.

Emotional stability will not erase pain. It teaches her how to process it without losing herself. She refuses to suppress her emotions or internalizes them as flaws. Instead, she honors her pain, feels it fully, and then releases it with intention. She understands that ignoring her pain does not heal it, acknowledging it does. Fears of heartbreak, disappointment, or grief, now gives room for emotional maturity. To walk through those experiences without allowing them to reshape her. Pain becomes a teacher, not a prison.

Having emotional stability does not eliminate conflict. It gives her the tools to handle it with intelligence. She understands that there is no need to avoid difficult conversations or sacrifice her truth to maintain false compatibility. She communicates openly because she trusts her voice. She sets boundaries early because she honors her wellbeing. She speaks the truth in love because emotional safety matters more than temporary comfort. Conflict no longer threatens her, it becomes an opportunity to clarify expectations, deepen understanding, or release what is no longer aligned.

Peace is not guaranteed when she is emotionally stable, but it makes peace possible. Peace stops being a condition of her environment and becomes a condition of her spirit. There is no need to wait for people, situations, or circumstances to change, but choose peace internally and guard it externally. She becomes selective about where she invests her time, energy, and emotions. She recognizes that peace is not found, it is cultivated. It is a discipline, a habit, and a spiritual practice.

She becomes the woman who is no longer moved by storms because she has learned to anchor herself from within. Her anchor is not external validation, temporary comfort, or unstable circumstances. Instead of spiraling into panic or shutting down emotionally, she approaches challenges with calm problem-solving, spiritual insight, and mental clarity.

The outcome of this mindset is profound: she becomes a woman whose presence carries peace, whose voice carries authority, whose decisions carry clarity, and whose life carries purpose.

She becomes a woman who changes the atmosphere of every room she enters. A woman who elevates her relationships, protects her boundaries, honors her emotions, follows God's guidance, and manifests the life she was created to live.

This is the transformation that happens when she chooses herself fully, intentionally, and unapologetically.

—— HER DECISION-MAKING UPGRADE

There is a profound shift that takes place inside a woman when she finally chooses to manifest herself first. It happens quietly at first. So quietly she may not even notice it. But slowly and steadily, her decision-making begins to transform. No longer shaped by fear, old wounds, or the voices of the past, her choices begin to rise from a deeper truth.

She begins to trust her no as much as her yes. She understands that not every opportunity is a blessing and not every delay is a rejection. She recognizes her intuition as divine guidance, not an inconvenience. She no longer needs loud signs or dramatic warnings to understand what is misaligned. Her spirit feels it instantly, her body senses it immediately, and her heart rejects it naturally.

This is the upgrade that happens when a woman finally returns to herself. She becomes impossible to mislead because she knows her truth and her worth. It is impossible to distract her, because she knows her direction. Her decisions sharpen not because life demands perfection, but because she refuses to continue living from emotional patterns she has already outgrown. She no longer let people, circumstances, or insecurity speak louder than her own spirit. She chooses from power, not panic.

Once a woman knows who she is, she stops letting confusion have the final say. Her peace speaks louder. And she listens fully, intentionally, and unapologetically.

This is the decision-making upgrade Manifest Me awakens within her. The ability to choose from her highest self instead of her wounded self. And once she begins making decisions from this place, her life can do nothing but rise to meet her.

— HER FINANCIAL AND ABUNDANCE SHIFT

Abundance is not just about money, it is about how a woman sees herself. It's what she believes she deserves, and what she gives herself permission to receive. Manifest Me teaches that the flow of abundance begins in the mind long before it ever reaches the bank account. It begins the moment a woman stops treating her worth like a negotiation and starts treating it like a standard. When a woman believes she is worthy, her entire financial world begins to shift. She moves differently in rooms. She speaks differently in opportunities. She walks differently toward her goals. She no longer shrinks to fit environments that do not honor her value. She won't apologize for wanting more, needing more, or expecting more. Her relationship with abundance transforms the moment she transforms her relationship with herself.

Before she manifests herself, she may tolerate jobs that drain her, opportunities that suffocate her, or wages that insult her talent. She may silence her aspirations because others told her she was asking for too much. It's possible for her to remain loyal to environments that undervalue her, because she doubts whether better exists. She may remain small because smallness feels safe. But once she begins the journey of Manifest Me, the woman she was can no longer contain the woman she is becoming. She begins to see abundance not as a luxury, but as her natural birthright. She realizes that settling is not humility, but self-abandonment. She understands that scarcity was never her portion. It was her conditioning. And she begins to experience the truth that when her mindset rises, her income rises with it.

Suddenly, the jobs she once accepted begin to feel misaligned. The pay she once tolerated begins to feel disrespectful. The environment she once adapted to, begins to feel too small for the woman she is. Her standards shift, and her financial life follows. This shift is not only practical; it is spiritual. When she upgrades her internal worthiness, she upgrades her external possibilities. She becomes magnetic in a new way, attracting opportunities that reflect the identity she now walks in. She becomes bold enough to ask for what she deserves. Confident enough to decline what does not honor her, and wise enough to recognize when a door is simply too small for her destiny.

Abundance flows most easily to a woman who believes she deserves it. It expands most naturally for a woman who refuses to choose from fear. It responds most powerfully to a woman who no longer betrays herself financially. Manifest Me becomes the foundation of this transformation, because abundance cannot land where unworthiness lives. It cannot grow where fear dominates. It cannot settle where a woman keeps shrinking. But when she finally decides she is worthy of more, her actions begin to align with that decision.

Negotiations are managed differently. She charges differently. Her expectations and the way she receives them are different. She stops talking herself out of opportunities and begins preparing herself for them. She won't view success as something she has to chase, and starts seeing it as something that naturally builds around a healed version of herself.

The woman who manifests herself first no longer experiences abundance as coincidence. Her abundance becomes the natural outcome of a healed internal world. Her financial rise becomes the reflection of her internal rise. Her opportunities expand because she expands. And when a woman finally understands who she is, her finances, career, and purpose follow suit. Manifest Me teaches her that abundance is not something she earns. It is something she aligns with, and alignment begins when she knows who she is.

—— THE LIFE THAT MANIFEST WHEN SHE CHOOSES HERSELF

There is nothing more powerful, more revolutionary, or more life-altering than the moment a woman finally chooses herself. Not in a moment of collapse or exhaustion, but in a moment of success. When she realizes that everything she has been praying for, fighting for, hoping for, and yearning for begins with the woman looking back at her in the mirror. Choosing yourself becomes the turning point. It is the quiet awakening that whispers, "I am no longer abandoning me." It is the sacred declaration that says, "I will no longer live beneath my truth." It is the internal shift that declares, "I am done shrinking for survival."

It is the moment your soul exhales and your spirit steps forward to reclaim the woman life tried to bury.

A woman who chooses herself becomes unstoppable. Not because the world suddenly becomes gentle or predictable, but because she is no longer moved by the storms that once destroyed her. She stops operating from fear, stops being shaped by trauma, and stops being imprisoned by old emotional patterns. She begins living from a place of power, and grounded in the truth of who she is. Her value no longer wavers in the presence of pressure. She is no longer emotionally tossed by the expectations of others. She becomes the woman her younger self needed: steady, wise, intuitive, whole, and free.

And when a woman chooses herself, her life responds in ways that feel almost supernatural. Opportunities don't just appear. The world around her begins to reflect the inner transformation happening within her. Relationships that once required her to earn love become undeserving of her time and energy. She begins attracting people who honor her boundaries, respect her voice, and match her emotional maturity. Chaos stops feeling familiar. Inconsistency stops feeling exciting. She craves stability because stability now lives inside her.

Peace becomes her new standard. Not a fleeting moment, but a daily rhythm. It flows more naturally because she is no longer manufacturing storms to feel worthy or alive. Her life becomes intentional. She wakes up with a clearer mind, a calmer spirit, and a deeper sense of direction. Peace stops being something she searches for and becomes something she carries within. And then joy returns. This joy is deeper, richer, and more sustainable because it comes from authenticity, not approval.

The most profound shift, however, is how she begins to see herself. Choosing herself reveals the power that has always been within her. She trusts her intuition with a confidence she didn't realize she possessed. She holds her emotions with compassion instead of criticism.

She evolves without apologizing for her growth. Guilt and shame lose their grip.

Her life becomes less about surviving and more about being. Less about pleasing others and more about honoring herself. Less about proving her worth and more about embodying it. She gains the courage to dismantle the versions of herself that were built from pain, fear, or expectations. She returns to the woman she was meant to be; confident, intuitive, grounded, radiant, powerful, and whole. She realizes the world does not need a smaller version of her. It needs the real her.

She invests in what multiplies her peace, her purpose, and her power. Life becomes more focused, more intentional, and more fulfilling. She no longer pours into dead situations out of fear or familiarity. She refuses to give her power to environments that do not honor who she is. Her selectivity becomes wisdom, not arrogance. And that wisdom elevates every part of her life.

Her productivity increases as inner chaos dissolves. Emotional grounding gives her the clarity to complete tasks without spiraling into overthinking, procrastination, or doubt. She becomes more intentional, more creative, and more capable. She no longer sabotages her own progress. She experiences results that once felt out of reach because she is no longer working against herself.

Her friendships deepen, her romantic connections become healthier, and her family interactions become clearer. Choosing herself removes the blind spots that once kept her loyal to unhealthy relationships. She sees people clearly and chooses wisely.

Financially, everything expands. When a woman chooses herself, she stops undervaluing her gifts. She stops taking roles that belittle her abilities. She stops viewing abundance as something meant for others but not for her. She becomes bold enough to walk away from what insults her value and brave enough to pursue what aligns with her purpose. Finances flow naturally because she no longer blocks it with guilt, fear, or unworthiness. Her mindset shifts from scarcity to overflow, and her life follows.

Spiritually, her connection to God deepens. Choosing herself places her in divine alignment. Her discernment sharpens. Her intuition strengthens. She begins recognizing God's guidance with clarity instead of confusion. Delays become redirection. Closed doors become protection. Peace becomes evidence of God's presence. She trusts the process, trusts the timing, and trusts the unfolding of her destiny.

Emotionally, she becomes anchored. She is no longer reactive; she is responsive. She becomes harder to offend, slower to panic, quicker to regulate. Her triggers lose their power because she has learned to understand them instead of fear them. She becomes emotionally safe within herself. A temple of peace rather than turmoil.

Mentally, she becomes clear and steady. She stops replaying old wounds. She stops predicting disaster. She no longer views life through the lens of insecurity. Her mind becomes a place of possibility, vision, and truth. She thinks courageously. She chooses intentionally, and dreams fearlessly.

And perhaps the greatest transformation of all is this: choosing herself makes her life feel fulfilling again. She stops performing for acceptance, hiding her softness, and apologizing for her power. She begins living from her soul instead of her survival patterns.

Her days feel lighter, her choices freer, her future possible again.

—— THE ESSENCE OF MANIFEST ME: THE RETURN TO MYSELF

The essence of Manifest Me is not found in a moment, a mantra, or a motivation high. It is found in the sacred unraveling of the woman you pretended to be and the sacred revealing of the woman you truly are. It is the journey of peeling back the layers that life forced you to wear. The layers of strength that became heavy, silence that became suffocating, fear that became familiar. Manifest Me is a homecoming, a return, a restoration. It is the moment a woman realizes she has been living as the edited version of herself. The version that was acceptable, and easy for others to digest. While the real her sat beneath the surface waiting to be acknowledged.

The essence of Manifest Me is alignment. When you are aligned internally, life begins to align externally. Doors open with ease. Relationships flow with clarity. Opportunities meet you without force. Peace settles into your spirit without effort. You stop chasing and begin attracting.

This journey is not about becoming someone new. It is about remembering someone ancient. The version of you untouched by heartbreak, untouched by fear, untouched by comparison, and untouched by the weight of proving yourself. It is the reawakening of the woman you were before life convinced you to shrink.

Manifest Me invites you to meet yourself at the deepest level. The woman with vision and desires. The woman with softness she forgot how to show, and brilliance she forgot how to honor. The powerful woman who recognizes the power that lives within.

Manifest Me is the invitation to stop abandoning your truth in exchange for belonging. It is the permission to choose yourself even when choosing yourself disrupts the narrative others created for you.

Manifest Me is the rebirth of a woman who finally realizes she is allowed to be powerful and peaceful, soft and strong, bold and grounded. She is allowed to evolve without explanation. She is allowed to release what no longer reflects her identity. She is allowed to claim a life that honors her. Manifest Me is the point where self-awareness becomes self-honor, where self-honor becomes self-worth, where self-worth becomes self-leadership, and where self-leadership becomes self-embodiment.

Manifest Me shifts the center of power back to where it belongs…..inside you.

This is the journey of being the woman you were always meant to be. The woman who no longer contorts herself to fit into rooms that cannot contain her. It is the moment you stop striving outward and begin rising inward. It is the moment you return to the woman you lost while trying to be everything for everyone else.

Manifest Me is the awakening of the woman who knows who she is, what she deserves, and what she will no longer allow. It is the moment your name, your voice, your spirit, and your presence reconnect. Manifest Me is not something you do. It is someone you are.

And once you have knowledge of her, your life will never, and can never be the same. This is the essence of Manifest Me: The sacred unraveling of everything you are not, so the unveiling of everything you are can finally begin.

CHAPTER 4

Attachment Styles & Manifestation Blocks

CHAPTER 4

ATTACHMENT STYLES & MANIFESTATION BLOCKS

 Your attachment style begins forming in the earliest chapters of your life long before you have words, awareness, or understanding. Childhood is where your nervous system first learns how to interpret the world. It's where your heart first learns what love feels like, your mind first learns what to expect from people, and your spirit first learns what it must do to stay emotionally safe. Attachment is not shaped in dramatic moments, but in the tiny, repeated experiences that imprint patterns onto your developing emotional world. These moments are subtle but powerful, It teaches you without anyone ever saying a word. It shows how the world will respond to your needs.

When you cried, your body recorded whether someone came to soothe you or whether you were left alone until your tears dried from exhaustion. When you reached out for comfort, you learned whether comfort meant being held or being pushed away. Times you expressed emotions, you were taught through tone, expression, or silence whether you would be met with understanding or irritation. And when you were hurt, you learned whether someone would help you make sense of the pain or whether you would be expected to figure it out alone. These early emotional interactions become lessons your nervous system memorizes, not lessons you consciously think about. They form the blueprint for your emotional world.

If your caregivers were consistently warm, present, and emotionally attuned, you learned that closeness is safe, that love is dependable, and that your needs matter. Your developing heart felt held. When you expressed emotions, they felt allowed. Your voice felt heard when you cried out. Safety was your foundation, and trust was something that came naturally. But if your caregivers were inconsistent; loving one moment, distant or overwhelmed the next, your nervous system learned to anticipate change. You never knew which version of love you would receive. You internalized the belief that affection was unstable and that you needed to work for attention or cling tightly to stay connected. You learned to chase love because somewhere inside you, it always felt like it might slip away.

If your caregivers were emotionally unavailable or dismissive, your nervous system learned to shrink your needs to survive. Those actions taught you that emotions were burdensome, that vulnerability led to disappointment, and that relying on others was risky. You became independent. Not because you were strong, but because you had no other choice. And if your caregivers were frightening, unpredictable, or unstable, your nervous system grew up in chaos. You longed for connection but feared it at the same time. You craved closeness but expected danger. Your spirit stayed on alert, unable to fully trust anyone, including yourself. Love became both the safest place you wanted to run to and the most dangerous place you needed to escape.

These early experiences taught you a silent emotional language. The language of whether you believe you matter, whether your emotions are allowed, whether you expect to be supported or abandoned, whether connection feels safe or overwhelming, and whether love feels nurturing or threatening. And because these lessons are learned before language, they become deeply embedded. They hide beneath your confidence, beneath your accomplishments, beneath your adulthood. They become instinct shaping how you love, trust, attach, cope, communicate, and interpret the behavior of others.

Attachment is not something you decide. It is something you absorb. It forms in the pauses between your needs and your caregivers' responses. It forms in the moments your spirit wonders, "Am I safe?" It forms in the emotional spaces where you learned, "This is what love feels like." In environments where you either felt protected, or learned to protect yourself.

And because attachment forms so early, it becomes the emotional foundation for every relationship you enter as an adult; including the relationship you have with yourself.

When you finally understand this, something sacred happens. You stop blaming yourself for your patterns. You stop judging yourself for the ways you've loved, and shaming yourself for the reactions you've had. You cease from criticizing the girl who did her best with the emotional tools she inherited. You begin to realize that your attachment style isn't evidence of your flaws. It is evidence of your early emotional experiences. And the moment you understand where your patterns came from, you finally gain the power to evolve them.

—— THE REALITY OF ATTACHMENT STYLES

Attachment styles are the emotional patterns that shape the way you love, trust, connect, and protect yourself. They form long before you understand what relationships are supposed to feel like or what emotional safety truly means. These early patterns become the blueprint your nervous system uses to navigate the world. They influence how you communicate, receive affection, respond to conflict, and what you subconsciously believe you deserve in connection. They quietly script your expectations. Whether you anticipate closeness or distance, safety or disappointment, nurturing or neglect. Without ever realizing it, your attachment style becomes the emotional language you speak, a language you learned long before you could form words.

This attachment blueprint becomes the internal script behind every relationship you enter. It determines whether you expect love or brace for abandonment, whether you lean in or pull away, whether you cling to connection or detach to protect yourself. It affects whether silence feels like peace or rejection. If conflict feels like intimacy or danger, and if you believe love must be earned through performance or simply received as your birthright. These patterns are not conscious decisions, but they are reflexes. They are survival responses your nervous system adopted in childhood. And because they are stored deep within your subconscious mind, they tend to appear automatically; especially in your closest and most vulnerable relationships.

Understanding your attachment style is one of the most powerful tools in Manifest Me because attachment determines how safe you feel inside yourself. Emotional safety is the foundation for every healthy decision you will ever make. If you do not feel safe internally, you cannot build safety externally. You cannot manifest healthy, aligned relationships if your nervous system only recognizes love through fear. It's difficult to attract a partnership that respects you, if your attachment patterns subconsciously pull you toward what is familiar instead of what is healthy. How can you experience emotional ease if you are constantly bracing for rejection, abandonment, or disappointment? When internal instability becomes your emotional default, it colors how you experience everything.

This is why attachment awareness is essential. It gives you language for your emotional reactions. It helps you understand why certain people feel magnetic and others feel overwhelmed. You understand why you repeat patterns even when they hurt. You see clearly why familiar chaos feels safer than unfamiliar peace. It allows you to recognize that your reactions are not random, they are rooted. And once you understand the roots, you finally gain the power to change the fruits.

Attachment awareness helps you evolve your patterns instead of being ruled by them. It allows you to respond consciously instead of reacting automatically. It guides you toward choosing partners who honor your needs instead of triggering your wounds. It empowers you to set boundaries without guilt, communicate without fear, and navigate conflict without collapsing. Most importantly, it helps you create emotional safety within yourself so you can finally experience emotional safety with others.

Understanding your attachment style brings compassion where blame once lived. Self judgment softens, and reactions are no longer viewed through shame. The girl who adapted to the emotional environment she was given no longer deserves criticism. That adaptation becomes understandable.

Attachment is revealed not as a flaw, but as a story and a narrative formed before there were tools to shape it. With that awareness comes power. The power to rewrite the script. As your story changes, authorship is reclaimed. A new emotional language is formed, and your relational world begins to transform in response.

—— THE HIDDEN SABOTEUR: HOW ATTACHMENT STYLES BLOCK YOUR MANIFESTATION

Attachment styles reach far beyond how love is expressed toward others. They influence self perception and shape the way the world is experienced. These styles create the lenses through which connection, intimacy, conflict, and safety are interpreted. Quietly, emotional expectations are formed and unspoken rules are followed without conscious awareness. In this way, attachment becomes the unseen narrator beneath daily choices, influencing boundaries, guiding relationships, and shaping the dreams believed to be possible. Growth is often blocked by what appears external. Like difficult people, disappointing circumstances, mistimed opportunities, or seasons that did not unfold as hoped. Yet the most significant barriers often live within. At the core are emotional patterns formed long before there was language to explain them or awareness to question their purpose. These patterns were not created to punish. Their origin was protection. But protection becomes limited when the threat has passed and the response remains.

Attachment styles quietly determine how far a woman will allow herself to rise, how deeply she believes she can receive love, how boldly she advocates for herself, and how confidently she steps into a room. They form her internal thermostat. Setting the temperature for what feels safe, what feels threatening, what feels familiar, and what feels overwhelming. A woman cannot fully embrace Manifest Me while her attachment wounds are quietly manifesting for her. She cannot evolve into her next level when her nervous system is still operating from the emotional memories of her past. She will not be able to rise into her highest self when her attachment patterns pull her back into old cycles.

Each attachment style creates its own internal cage. Not a physical cage, but a cage made of memory, lessons childhood taught her about love, and emotional rules she created to survive. Rooted in the fear that being fully herself might cost her connection. These invisible cages determine how deeply she trusts, how she communicates, how she chooses partners, how she responds to conflict, and how she perceives her own worth. They influence whether she embraces experiences in her life or sabotages it. They shape whether she moves toward wholeness or clings to what is familiar, even when familiar is painful.

To truly understand how these patterns keep a woman stuck, we must go deeper into the heart, the mind, and the soul of the matter. Only then can she begin rewriting the emotional blueprint that has shaped her life for far too long.

—— THE CORE TRUTH: ATTACHMENT WOUNDS MANIFEST BEFORE HEALING

Every woman carries an internal realm; a sacred inner landscape shaped by memories, patterns, fears, hopes. This becomes an emotional blueprint established long before she understood the meaning of safety. This internal realm is deeply spiritual. It is powerful, creative, prophetic, and magnetic. It holds the echoes of her past and the seeds of her future. And if she does not intentionally partner with God to shape it, that inner realm will shape her life on its own.

Attachment wounds, in particular, are not passive. They do not sit quietly in the background waiting for an invitation to influence her journey. Instead, they manifest before she does. Attachment wounds utter words before her healed self has a chance to speak. These wounds choose from fear before her confidence learns to choose from truth. They whisper familiar narratives before her evolving identity has the opportunity to rewrite the script.

If a woman does not intentionally manifest herself, her attachment wounds will manifest her life for her. She will select partners who reflect her unhealed beliefs. Wounds will dictate the boundaries she sets, or fails to set. There comes a determination whether she speaks her truth or silences it. She will shape her confidence, often without her awareness, that influences her decisions and emotional reactions. The reactions that pull her back into cycles that feel familiar, even when those cycles are painful. It becomes easy for her to believe these patterns are simply "who I am," when in reality, they are injuries. Attachment wounds learned their lessons early, and because they learned them early, they operate with authority that feels believable.

A woman may long for love, but if her wounds learned that love is unpredictable, she will subconsciously sabotage intimacy when it becomes real. She may say she deserves respect, but if her wounds learned that respect is conditional, she will tolerate what diminishes her.

She has dreams of rising higher, but if her wounds associate success with abandonment, she will unconsciously hold herself back. In these moments, her wounds slip into the driver's seat. Her wounds become the storyteller and the gatekeeper between who she was and who she could become.

This is why Manifest Me is not simply a practice. It is a reclaiming. It is the moment a woman takes back authorship of her life. She makes the decision to stop allowing old emotional patterns to dictate her worth, her relationships, or her destiny. The declaration "I will no longer allow who I had to be, determine who I am allowed to become." Manifest Me teaches a woman to step into the position her wounds have been occupying. It shifts her from reaction to intention. It also teaches her to choose her future from her healed self instead of her hurt self. Empowerment is to build boundaries based on worth rather than fear, and evaluate relationships from clarity instead of desperation.

This process is not about blame. It is about liberation. Not about pointing fingers at the past, but reclaiming the pen that writes her future. Understanding your attachment style becomes the beginning of this awakening. It is the moment you stop fighting yourself without knowing why. You gain language for your inner world and clarity about what has been driving your relationships, choices, and emotional responses. When you understand your attachment style, you finally understand the blueprint you have unconsciously been living from. And once you understand the blueprint, you gain the power to redesign it.

Awareness becomes the birthplace of renewed lifestyle. It becomes the first breath of a new identity. Awareness is the quiet revolution that shifts everything. When you finally see how your attachment wounds have been manifesting your life, you can choose to step into your becoming with intention.

You can choose to manifest yourself. Not the version created by survival, but the version formed by healing. This is where true becoming begins: the moment you decide to rise above the emotional blueprint you inherited and create the identity you were always destined to embody.

CHAPTER 5

Anxious Attachment

CHAPTER 5

ANXIOUS ATTACHMENT

 A woman with anxious attachment often carries the emotional residue of inconsistency. In her past, love may have been unpredictable. Sometimes nurturing, sometimes distant, sometimes comforting, or sometimes chaotic. Because of this, she learned to monitor, chase, and overextend to keep love close.

An anxious woman feels deeply. Her emotions tend to be intense, and her fears of abandonment often sit beneath the surface of her interactions. She may overthink every silence, every gesture, and every delayed response. She attaches quickly because she longs for stability, but the longing comes from a place of fear rather than emotional stability.

In relationships, she gives more than she receives. Often believing that her effort can compensate for someone else's lack. She confuses anxiety with connection and passion with connection or compatibility. She loses herself trying to hold onto others and often interprets distance as danger.

This attachment style deeply affects manifestation. When you fear losing love, you call in situations that reflect your fear. You attract partners who confirm your insecurities or relationships that require you to work for love. You settle because you dread the idea of being alone. Your self-worth becomes entangled in someone else's presence.

To break free from anxious attachment, you must learn to trust yourself more than you fear abandonment. You must stop rescuing people who show you they are emotionally unavailable.

You must build a life, identity, and peace that are not dependent on anyone's validation.

Anxious attachment creates a reality where a woman is always looking outward instead of inward. She becomes emotionally tethered to the reactions, moods, and behaviors of the people around her. Without realizing it, she begins to rely on others to tell her who she is, how valuable she is, and whether she is worthy of staying. Her sense of safety depends on something outside of herself; a partner's tone, a friend's reassurance, a parent's approval, or a coworker's praise.

She is constantly scanning the room, conversations, subtle shifts in someone's energy. Trying to determine whether she is still accepted, wanted, or loved. It's not because she is needy. It's because somewhere in her story, consistency was unpredictable and love was unreliable. At a young age, she learned she had to "earn" closeness. So she over-performs, over-gives, and over-extends, because deep inside, she feels she is not enough as she is.

An anxious woman becomes addicted to external validation because she has never been taught to validate herself. She looks to others for emotional regulation. No one ever modeled what emotional safety feels like inside her own body. She has learned how to calm others, but not herself. She can soothe everyone else's storms, but not the one within her.

She forgets that her own spirit holds the wisdom, stability she seeks. She forgets that the love she is chasing is a reflection of the love she has not yet learned to give herself.

—— HER NERVOUS SYSTEM LIVES IN SURVIVAL MODE

The anxious woman cannot fully manifest herself because she is always searching for emotional danger, even when no danger is present. Her nervous system stays in a constant state of watching, waiting, and anticipating what could go wrong. This hypervigilance is exhausting, yet it feels normal to her because the emotional chaos mirrors the climate she grew up in. Even when life is peaceful, her body does not trust the calm. Even when love is steady, her heart does not trust the closeness. When circumstances are stable, her mind is still uncertain of the safety. Not because she is pessimistic, but because her body remembers what inconsistency felt like, long after her mind has tried to forget.

Her childhood may have taught her that love comes. but only sometimes. That she matters, but not consistently. She is seen, but only when it's convenient for someone else. These early lessons embed themselves in her nervous system, creating a blueprint of unpredictability that follows her into adulthood. So, she enters relationships braced for loss, silence, abandonment, and emotional shifts that may never actually occur.

Her spirit wants love, and emotional intimacy, but her body prepares for danger. She longs for closeness, yet anticipates withdrawal. Her heart reaches out, but her nervous system pulls back. This internal tug-of-war keeps her trapped between who she wants to become and the safety strategies she learned as a child. It is not a lack of desire for healing. It is the presence of emotional wounds that still speak louder than her evolving identity.

— SHE BUILDS HER LIFE AROUND OTHERS INSTEAD OF HERSELF

An anxious woman does not prioritize herself. She prioritizes attachment. Her emotional compass is not guided by what is healthy, aligned, or true, but by what keeps people close. She builds her entire inner life around maintaining connection, even when the cost is her sense of self. She pours excessively so no one leaves. She bends her boundaries to avoid upsetting others, and becomes agreeable as a shield against conflict. She becomes endlessly available so she won't be forgotten, while forgiving prematurely so she doesn't risk losing connection. She chooses presence over peace, attention over alignment, and relationship over self-respect. This is not because she lacks strength or self-worth, but because she has been conditioned since childhood to fear loss more deeply than she fears self-betrayal.

For the anxious woman, attachment becomes a survival strategy. She does not instinctively ask, "Is this good for me?" She asks, "Will they stay?" Even as an adult, she makes others comfortable by softening her truth to avoid being misunderstood, or sacrificing her needs to remain connected. She fears that if she stands in her fullness, she will be too much. If she expresses her needs, she will be a burden. If she sets a boundary, she will be abandoned. So, she betrays herself long before anyone else ever gets the chance.

Going deeper, this pattern creates an emotional life built on imbalance. She invests more than she receives and carries more weight than she should. The anxious woman apologizes for things that are not her fault. She rationalizes behavior that hurts her, and loves from fear rather than from security. She becomes overly attuned to the moods of others, while scanning constantly for signs of withdrawal or rejection. Her entire emotional world becomes a cycle of anticipating, accommodating, and adjusting herself to maintain attachment. In the process, she loses sight of her own needs, desires, and worthiness.

Spiritually, this burden is even heavier. She begins to mistake people-pleasing for humility. Emotionally overworking for love, and self-sacrificing for loyalty, becomes a norm.

The anxious woman equates suffering with devotion, as if her willingness to endure, proves her value. She struggles to hear God's voice over the loudness of her anxiety, because her body is always braced for what might go wrong. She cannot fully receive divine love or divine promises, because she is always caught in the tension of keeping earthly connections intact.

This is why the anxious woman often feels depleted and invisible despite giving so much. Why she feel unappreciated despite pouring endlessly. Her love is real, intentions are pure, heart is soft, but her attachment patterns drown her truth. She does not yet understand that connection without self-respect is bondage, and love that requires self-erasure is not love at all.

Her anxious patterns are not reflections of her character. They are reflections of her conditioning. She was taught that survival depends on staying connected, even if the cost is her soul. But the deeper truth is this, she was never meant to lose herself to be loved. Never intended to bend to maintain proximity, or sacrifice her needs to preserve relationships built on fear.

When an anxious woman begins healing, she learns to prioritize identity over attachment. She learns that she is allowed to take up space. She discovers that losing people who cannot honor her truth is not loss. It is liberation. And gradually, she begins to understand that the version of her who once betrayed herself was not weak, but she was simply doing what she needed to feel safe.

Healing teaches her that true safety comes from within, not from chasing connections. It teaches her that self-respect is not a risk, but a requirement. And it reveals something life-changing: when she no longer betrays herself, she becomes impossible to abandon.

—— HOW THIS STOPS HER FROM MANIFESTING HER NEXT LEVEL

An anxious attachment style quietly blocks a woman from manifesting her next level because it keeps her anchored to fear. Manifestation requires clarity, confidence, emotional grounding, and the ability to move from intentions. But anxious attachment trains a woman to move from panic. It conditions her to chase connection instead of standing firmly in her own worth. Instead of focusing on her purpose, she focuses on people. Rather than listening to God's voice, she listens for signs of withdrawal. Instead of trusting her path, she fears losing what she has. Her energy becomes scattered, and her spirit becomes unsettled. All of which disrupt the alignment required to step into her next dimension.

This attachment style keeps her in a constant state of internal instability. It tells her that safety comes from other people, not from within. It convinces her that her value is tied to how much she gives, how available she is, or how well she can keep others pleased. But manifestation requires the opposite. It requires a rooted belief that you are whole and worthy. Not because someone chooses you, but because God already has. When a woman is anxiously attached, she cannot access this inner stillness. Her mind races, her spirit braces, and her body prepares for an emotional impact that may not even exist. This emotional turbulence disrupts her ability to discern clearly.

It also disrupts manifestation because it magnifies misalignment. A woman who fears abandonment will cling to relationships that drain her, opportunities that limit her, and environments that shrink her. She will mistake familiarity for safety, even when familiarity is the very thing delaying her elevation. Manifestation requires release. It requires the courage to let go of what no longer lines up. But anxious attachment interprets releasing as losing, and losing as danger. So she stays attached to what God has been trying to remove. She holds on to what her spirit has outgrown. She tries to resuscitate what is already dead. In doing so, she delays the blessings waiting for her because her hands are too full of fear to receive what is meant for her future.

This attachment undermines her self-trust, which is the very foundation of manifestation. In order to manifest at a higher level, a woman must trust her intuition, her boundaries, her voice, her emotions, and her discernment. But anxious attachment makes her doubt everything. It tells her she is imagining things. It says she is too sensitive and to silence herself, that pushes her to seek reassurance outside of herself instead of listening to the wisdom God placed inside of her. When she cannot trust herself, she cannot trust the path God is unfolding for her. And when she cannot trust the path, she cannot walk into her next season with authority.

Spiritually, anxious attachment creates interference. It becomes an emotional static that blocks divine clarity. It makes her react before she can receive, and chase before she can hear. God calls her to be still, but anxiety calls her to strive. God calls her to step boldly, but anxiety calls her to shrink and attach. She cannot fully manifest her next level while allowing fear-driven patterns to guide her decisions more than faith-driven truth.

Ultimately, anxious attachment delays elevation, because it keeps a woman rooted in who she had to be. She is continuously tied to survival strategies that once protected her, but now imprisons her. Manifestation cannot occur inside emotional prisons, it requires spiritual and emotional stability.

The moment she begins healing her anxious attachment, everything shifts. Her spirit steadies and her mind clears. She petitions prayers that align with her purpose instead of her fears. She no longer chases what is not meant for her, or fears losing what is predestined for her. She becomes a woman who can manifest with power because she is no longer manifesting from panic; she is manifesting from truth.

That is when her next level finally becomes accessible.

—— HOW THE ANXIOUS WOMAN SHOWS UP IN EVERYDAY LIFE

An anxious woman shows up in everyday life with a tenderness that is often misunderstood. A tenderness shaped not by weakness, but by wounds that taught her to earn love instead of receiving it freely. She rereads her text messages, not because she is obsessive, but because she fears she may have said something wrong that could push someone away. She apologizes excessively, even for things she did not do, because her nervous system is conditioned to keep peace at any cost. She says "yes" when everything inside her is begging her to say "no," because rejection feels more dangerous than resentment. She double-books herself, overcommits, and burns herself out trying to support everyone but herself, believing that her value is tied to her usefulness.

In her interactions, she feels devastated when someone's tone shifts or energy changes, immediately assuming she is the cause. A delayed response becomes a sign of disinterest. A shorter text becomes a sign of irritation. A pause in communication becomes evidence of abandonment. She worries she is being replaced the moment someone pulls back even slightly. Not because she lacks intelligence, but because her body carries old memories of losing connection without warning. She stays in relationships long after they have expired. Clinging to broken spaces because the pain of leaving feels more terrifying than the pain of staying. Unfortunately, familiar hurt feels safer than unfamiliar healing.

She gives love like a flood; generously, consistently, wholeheartedly. But she receives love like a drip; rationing the affection she allows herself to absorb, because she fears it will be taken away. She has learned to pour, but not to be poured into. The anxious woman has learned to give, but not to receive. She carries a constant sense of responsibility for the emotions of others, believing that if she loves hard enough, stays available enough, or tries perfectly enough, she can protect herself from abandonment.

What she does not yet understand is that her deep longing to be chosen is not proof that something is wrong with her. It is proof that she has not fully chosen herself. Her attachment wounds make her believe that connection must be maintained through self-sacrifice.

But the truth is, that choosing herself is what will finally allow her to step into relationships that reflect the love she has always deserved. Her anxious patterns are not a reflection of her worth, but a reflection of the emotional environments that shaped her. And as she heals, she will learn that she no longer has to beg for belonging, perform for love, or shrink to be accepted. Choosing herself becomes the beginning of her liberation.

—— SHE SHRINKS SO OTHERS FEEL COMFORTABLE

When a woman carries anxious attachment, she often convinces herself that her greatness is too loud. She feels as though her needs are too heavy, and her emotions are too much. The anxious woman learns to believe that shrinking herself makes her easier to love, as if reducing her brilliance will somehow make people stay. She tells herself that dimming her light will prevent others from feeling intimidated. As if softening her voice will keep her accepted, and lowering her expectations will keep her from being left alone. In response, she becomes a careful version of herself; not her true self, but her tolerated self. She becomes agreeable because disagreement feels dangerous. Adapting starts to be a norm, because expressing preferences feels risky. She becomes low-maintenance, because needing something feels like a burden. Her actions are emotionally flexible, so others never feel inconvenienced. She edits herself in real time, constantly adjusting to maintain peace, connection, or approval.

But shrinking does not create safety. It creates invisibility. It erases her identity piece by piece, until she no longer recognizes herself outside of the roles she plays for others. It teaches people to love her mask instead of her truth. So, she learns to prioritize comfort over authenticity. The more she shrinks, the more disconnected she becomes from the woman she is created to be. Her voice becomes quiet, her desires become distant, and her intuition becomes muted. And slowly, she begins to believe that the reduced version of herself is all she is capable of offering.

Spiritually, shrinking blocks her from stepping into the abundance God designed for her. She cannot walk in divine purpose while trying to make everyone else comfortable.

She's unable to carry the fullness of her calling, while folding herself into spaces that require her to be less. She cannot hear God clearly when she is too busy managing the emotions of others. Shrinking keeps her loyal to environments that were never meant to hold her destiny. It keeps her tied to relationships that only benefit from her silence, and living at the level of her fear instead of the level of her anointing.

A woman cannot manifest her highest self while making herself small enough to fit inside relationships that were never worthy of her fullness. Her next level requires expansion, not contraction. Clarity, not confusion. It requires courage, but not appeasement. Healing teaches her that her voice does not threaten the right people, her emotions do not burden those who are meant for her, and her needs do not push away those who truly value her. When she stops shrinking, she stops abandoning herself. And when she stops abandoning herself, she becomes powerful and free. Finally able to manifest the woman she was always destined to become.

—— HER HEARTBREAK ISN'T FROM LOVERS; IT'S FROM SELF ABANDONMENT

Her heartbreak is rarely rooted in the people who walked away. It is rooted in the ways she walked away from herself. The anxious woman often believes that the individuals who disappointed her, betrayed her, or failed to love her properly, are the source of her deepest wounds. But the truth beneath the surface is far more profound. Her greatest heartbreak comes from the moments she betrayed herself in an attempt to keep others close. She gives away the very things she needs in hopes that someone will finally reciprocate. She abandons her feelings to avoid discomfort. The anxious woman sacrifices her boundaries because she fears that enforcing them will push people away. For this reason, she slowly loses herself in the name of love; believing that if she becomes small enough, selfless enough, or pleasing enough, someone will finally stay.

But the loss she fears most is not actually someone leaving her. The loss that devastates her spirit is the loss of her own identification. The identity she keeps sacrificing piece by piece, every time she chooses attachment over alignment.

This is the heartbreak that lingers long after the relationship ends. The heartbreak that follows her into new seasons that keeps her tied to cycles she was meant to outgrow. She grieves the parts of herself she abandoned. The woman who had a voice and boundaries. The woman who once dreamed boldly before fear silenced her.

This self-abandonment is what blocks her manifestation more than anything external ever could. Manifestation requires a grounded woman who knows who she is, what she deserves, and where God is leading her. But anxious attachment creates an identity wrapped in fear instead of truth. It tells her that love must be earned, safety must be watched for, and belonging must be maintained at any cost. It conditions her to seek affirmation from others rather than from God. To build her sense of self through relationships, instead of from the inside out. With every act of self-betrayal, her spiritual footing becomes less stable. She becomes disconnected from the very bond required for elevation.

Anxious attachment fragments her alignment. Peace is at war within her own spirit. She cannot manifest clarity when she is constantly suppressing her needs. She is not capable of manifesting abundance when she is living in survival mode. She cannot manifest healthy relationships while abandoning herself inside unhealthy ones. When her foundation is rooted in fear of rejection rather than assurance of worth, she sacrifices her future, and her ability to rise.

Spiritually, this becomes a disconnect between her and God's design for her. God cannot elevate a woman who keeps shrinking. It's difficult to heal a woman who keeps hiding. He cannot pour into a woman whose hands are already full of people she is trying to keep from leaving. Self-abandonment closes the very doors that healing could open. It dims the light God is trying to shine through her, and blocks the blessings that require her to stand boldly.

The healing begins when she realizes that her heartbreak is not about who left. It's about the parts of herself she left behind. And the moment she begins choosing herself again, her confidence returns, and her manifestation power activates. Because a woman who no longer abandons herself becomes unstoppable. She is finally free to manifest the life she was designed to live.

THE TURNING POINT: WHEN ANXIOUS WOMEN BEGIN TO AWAKEN

The turning point for an anxious woman is not loud or dramatic. It is a quiet but life-altering awakening within her. It is when she begins to see herself clearly, and not through the distorted lens of rejection. She starts to realize that she is not hard to love. She has simply poured herself into people who were emotionally unavailable or unequipped to love her with the depth she gives so freely. She understands that she is not too emotional. She is a woman whose feelings were never validated, honored, or held with care. She recognizes that she is not clingy. She was conditioned to fear abandonment because consistency was not something she could rely on. She sees that she is not insecure by nature. She was shaped by environments that taught her to question herself. She accepts that she is not needy. She is a woman healing from a childhood, where her needs were minimized, ignored, or unmet.

This awakening shifts everything. When she finally stops trying to extract validation from people who could never give it. The capacity is not there, because they are wrestling with their own emotional limitations. She no longer performs for affection, or overextends for connection. Instead, she starts turning inward; toward her truth, her worthiness, her voice, her healing, and her God who never stops loving her even when others do.

Spiritually, this marks a divine turning point. She begins to see herself through God's eyes; chosen, worthy, whole, and deeply loved. She stops believing the lie that she must chase love. Her prayers shift from "Lord, let them stay" to "Lord, align me with what honors my soul." Her spirit, once consumed with fear, begins to breathe again.

This awakening is the birthplace of her becoming. She starts walking, showing up, and choosing differently. She becomes the woman who no longer fears abandonment because she has finally chosen herself. She's the woman who no longer questions her worth because she knows it is non-negotiable. The woman without a need to cling to relationships that hurts her, because she understands that letting go is not loss; it is liberation.

CHAPTER 6

Dismissive Avoidant Attachment

CHAPTER 6

DISMISSIVE AVOIDANT ATTACHMENT

 A woman with avoidant attachment learned early that vulnerability equals risk. She grew up in environments where emotional needs were dismissed, minimized, or met with inconsistency. She learned to rely on herself because depending on others felt unsafe or disappointing. Avoidant women often appear confident, independent, and self-sufficient, but beneath that strength is a deep fear of being fully seen. They create emotional distance as a form of protection. When someone gets too close, they retreat. When intimacy becomes real, they shut down. They avoid conflict or difficult conversations, because they fear losing control or exposing their emotional world. They maintain relationships at arm's length. Not because they don't want closeness, but because closeness feels overwhelming to their nervous system.

This attachment style sabotages manifestation in a quiet but powerful way. You may desire love but fear what true intimacy requires. You crave connection, but reject it the moment it begins to feel authentic. You find yourself pushing away emotionally available partners, while gravitating toward those who are distant. Because distance feels familiar, predictable, and safe. You tell yourself you prefer independence, but deep down you fear that if someone truly sees you; your softness, your needs, your emotions, they might reject you, or worse, abandon you. So you preemptively withdraw to protect your heart, not realizing that this self-protection also prevents you from receiving the blessings meant for you.

— THE WOMAN WHO FEARS WHAT SHE CRAVES

The woman with avoidant attachment lives in a constant emotional paradox. She deeply craves intimacy, yet fears the very closeness her heart longs for. Avoidant attachment creates a life where she stays close enough to feel connected, but distant enough to feel safe. She masters the art of controlling her emotions, guarding her inner world, and maintaining emotional distance. Not because she is cold or detached, but because vulnerability once led to disappointment or emotional danger. She learned early that needing others created discomfort. Expressing emotions will lead to dismissal or mockery. Vulnerability invited inconsistency instead of comfort, and that reaching out only made her feel exposed in ways her childhood never protected. In response, she adapted. She became the woman who "doesn't need anyone," the woman who always holds herself together. She is the reliable one, composed one, and the strong one. She becomes her own safe space, because no one ever taught her how to be safe with another person.

Avoidant women are profoundly misunderstood. People often think they lack emotion or depth, but the truth is the opposite. She feels deeply, loves intensely, and she cares more than she will ever admit out loud. Her distance is not emotional emptiness; it is emotional self-protection. The dismissive-avoidant woman is not detached because she doesn't feel. She is detached because she feels everything, and fears being consumed by it. Her independence is not always empowerment; sometimes it is armor. She fears being vulnerable because vulnerability was never met with safety. She struggles to trust anyone, because trust was never consistently modeled.

Spiritually, this creates a barrier between her and the life God is calling her into. She cannot manifest divine love while resisting human intimacy, or step into purpose while avoiding connection. It's difficult to receive blessings while guarding herself against being seen. Avoidant attachment does not just affect relationships. It affects alignment. It creates a life where she controls everything to avoid being hurt, but that same control prevents her from receiving what she has prayed for.

She longs for partnership but feels suffocated when it arrives. She wants emotional safety but mistrusts it when it's offered. Closeness is interpreted as a threat.

The avoidant woman must learn that safety does not come from walls. It comes from healing. Vulnerability is not a loss of power, but an expansion of it. She must learn that love does not have to overwhelm her; it can hold her. It's essential to know that being seen is not dangerous; it is divine. Manifest Me invites her to soften her defenses, test small acts of emotional openness, unlearn the belief that she must do everything alone, and to slowly let the right people into the spaces she has protected for so long. As she heals, her heart becomes less guarded. She can experience deeper connections and her relationships can become more stable. She becomes a woman who no longer fears what she craves, but receives it fully, boldly, and without apology.

—— SHE PROTECTS HERSELF THROUGH EMOTIONAL DISTANCE

A dismissive avoidant woman does not protect herself by shutting down because she is cold. She protects herself because she is cautious. She is not a heartless woman, but is heavily guarded. Others believe she is uninterested, when she is unsure if interest is emotionally safe. Her childhood likely taught her subtle but powerful messages: Your emotions overwhelm me, so handle it yourself. You're too sensitive, and I don't know how to comfort you. I am here physically, but not in the way you truly need. These early experiences create a silent emotional script inside her. Over time, she begins to internalize a belief that feels protective but ultimately becomes dangerous. The inside thoughts are, "If I don't rely on anyone, no one can hurt me."

This belief shapes everything. Slowly, she disconnects from her own emotional needs, because they were never honored. She disconnects from vulnerability because it never brought comfort.

She disconnects from the softer parts of herself; the parts that once wanted to be held, understood, and cared for, because those parts felt like liabilities in her early world. She disconnects from the idea that she can depend on anyone, because depending on others once led to disappointment, confusion, or emotional abandonment. What began as a survival strategy becomes a way of life.

By adulthood, emotional self-protection becomes her default operating system. She values independence above intimacy, because independence feels predictable and controllable. She feels safest when no one gets too close, because closeness stirs a fear she rarely admits. The fear that she won't know how to meet someone emotionally, or worse, that someone will get close enough to see the tender parts she has spent her life covering. She trusts herself far more than she will ever trust anyone else. Not out of arrogance, but out of necessity. She relies on logic because feelings feel unmanageable. And in this protective stance, she becomes the woman who sleeps with emotional armor on. She is guarded even in her dreams. Holding herself tightly because no one ever held her the way she needed.

Her distance is not the absence of feeling; it is the presence of fear. And while this distance shields her from pain, it also shields her from connection, intimacy, and the fullness of love she quietly longs for.

—— HER NERVOUS SYSTEM REJECTS VULNERABILITY

A woman with avoidant attachment doesn't run from relationships themselves, she runs from emotional exposure. Exposure feels dangerous because it requires her to open the very parts of herself that were never protected, nurtured, or affirmed. What she is truly avoiding is the possibility of disappointment, the weight of emotional obligation, and the vulnerability of depending on someone who may not consistently show up. Her nervous system reacts to closeness with the same intensity that an anxious woman feels when someone pulls away. While the anxious woman spirals when connection feels distant, the avoidant woman spirals when connection feels too close.

To her, emotional intimacy does not feel like safety; it feels like pressure. It feels like an expectation or losing control.

It feels like stepping into a space where she may have to reveal emotions she has spent her entire life containing. It feels like becoming vulnerable without any guarantee that her vulnerability will be honored or understood. Her body remembers what it was like to express a need and it not be met. It remembers the discomfort of being unseen or misunderstood. Her body remembers the emotional loneliness of childhood. When she had no choice but to self-soothe, stay strong, and shut down what felt too big for others to handle.

So when someone tries to get close, her nervous system sounds an alarm. She may withdraw emotionally, avoid deep conversations, redirect vulnerability with humor, or suddenly crave space. Her mind frames this distance as "logic" or "independence," but in reality, it is protection. Protection from being hurt in the same ways she once was. Vulnerability doesn't feel like a connection to her. It feels like exposure without insurance. And until she learns how to recognize and regulate this response, closeness will always feel like a risk her body cannot afford to take, even if her heart longs for it.

⎯ SHE BUILDS HER LIFE AROUND INDEPENDENCE INSTEAD OF INTIMACY

Avoidant attachment teaches a woman to build her life around independence, not as a conscious preference but as a protective strategy that once kept her emotionally safe. She learns early that the surest way to avoid disappointment is to avoid dependence altogether. So, she becomes her own provider, protector, and emotional anchor. She takes pride in needing nothing, wanting nothing, and relying on no one because this self-sufficiency feels secure. It feels like control. It feels like power, but this power is rooted in fear. As a result, she gravitates toward relationships that demand very little from her. She chooses partners who won't push for closeness, or ask too many emotional questions. She is comfortable with connecting with someone who won't require her to unravel her inner world. She prefers connections with wide emotional margins, because closeness feels like a threat to the stability she built within herself.

When relationships begin requiring emotional depth; the kind that demands vulnerability, openness, and emotional presence, she instinctively retreats.

Not because she lacks the desire for intimacy, but because intimacy forces her to confront feelings she has spent years suppressing. She avoids conflict not because she doesn't care, but because conflict exposes emotional needs she doesn't know how to express. She ends relationships quickly or distances herself gradually whenever she senses that someone is beginning to truly see her. She may convince herself that she prefers casual connections or that deep relationships are "too much work," but beneath that narrative lies a deeper truth: She longs for intimacy, but fears the emotional unraveling required to experience it.

Over time, she suppresses her needs so thoroughly that she begins to believe she doesn't have any. She becomes so accustomed to being her own emotional world, that she forgets how to let someone else in. But emotional independence rooted in avoidance is not real strength. It is survival dressed as self-sufficiency. True strength is the courage to be seen, the willingness to be held, and the openness to share emotional space with another person. Until the avoidant woman confronts the fear beneath her independence, she will continue choosing distance over the intimacy she secretly craves.

—— HOW AVOIDANCE STOPS HER FROM MANIFESTING HER NEXT LEVEL

Avoidant attachment becomes a barrier to manifesting a woman's next level because the very growth she desires requires openness, and openness is the thing her nervous system has been trained to fear. Manifesting Me calls a woman into emotional expansion, and the ability to receive love, support, partnership, opportunity, and divine alignment. But for the avoidant woman, receiving feels foreign, uncomfortable, and even threatening, because she has spent her entire life surviving by depending solely on herself. Her spirit longs for connection, but her conditioning rejects it. Manifestation requires vulnerability, the courage to be seen, known, and emotionally available, yet avoidant attachment teaches her to hide her most tender truths behind emotional walls. She prays for elevation, but elevation requires trust; trusting God's timing, the people He sends, and even herself enough to soften. Yet to her nervous system, trust feels dangerous because it once led to disappointment.

Her next level requires a heart opened enough to receive what she has been asking for, but avoidant attachment kept unreachable. Her next level requires connection; soul-aligned relationships, spiritual support, meaningful sisterhood, but avoidance keeps her distant from the very people positioned to bless her. Her next level requires embodiment. The courage to live fully in her emotions. That means allowing herself to feel deeply enough to transform. Avoidant women often manifest loneliness, not because they want it, but because emotional self-protection forms an accidental barrier against the very abundance their spirit is calling for.

Avoidant attachment also blocks manifestation because it disrupts her ability to receive guidance and spiritual alignment. Manifestation is not just desire, but it is partnership with God. But avoidance teaches her to rely only on her own strength, her own logic, and her own plans. She trusts her mind but not her spirit. She leans on her independence, but not divine support. Wants the promises of God, but resists the process. She asks for clarity but avoids the stillness required to hear God's voice. Prays for alignment, but protects herself from the intimacy required to walk in it. Spiritual elevation requires surrender and willingness, yet avoidance interprets surrender as loss of control. So, she manifests from self-protection instead of spiritual partnership, which limits her growth and minimizing what God is trying to release to her.

Avoidance causes her to manifest opportunities that match her emotional distance. She chooses relationships that feel "safe" because they require little vulnerability. She attracts partners who cannot love deeply because they mirror the emotional withholding she learned to normalize. She ends up in careers where vulnerability is unnecessary, even if they stifle her purpose. She gravitates toward environments that does not challenge her emotional armor. Avoidance doesn't just affect love, it affects purpose, finances, creativity, leadership, and spiritual calling. Her next level requires her to be fully present, fully expressed, fully open, but avoidance keeps her living half-present, half-expressed, and half-alive.

The avoidant woman also blocks her manifestation because it disconnects her from emotional truth. But manifestation is built on truth. She cannot call in abundance while pretending she doesn't need connection. It's difficult to attract aligned love while denying that she cares deeply. She cannot step into purpose while avoiding the emotional healing required to hold it.

Manifestation responds to authenticity, not performance. But avoidance convinces her to hide her deepest needs; even from herself. She may present herself as strong and self-contained, but manifestation sees the truth beneath the armor. She is a woman longing to be held, understood, and emotionally met. Until she acknowledges that truth, her manifestations remain limited, delayed, or even blocked.

Avoidant attachment sabotages her next level because it disrupts her ability to receive the foundation of abundance. Manifestation is not just about asking; it is about allowing, and allowing requires inner space. But avoidance creates emotional tightness, mental over-control, and spiritual resistance. Instead of receiving with ease, she analyzes, questions, and pulls away. It's challenging accepting blessings, because she second-guesses them. Avoidance tells her, "If I don't get too close, I can't get hurt," but what she doesn't realize is that distance also keeps her from receiving joy, intimacy, purpose, and overflow.

On an even deeper spiritual level, avoidant attachment blocks her intimacy with God. Avoidant women often struggle to pray vulnerably, surrender openly, or trust divine timing, because those acts require emotional closeness. She may trust God intellectually, but not emotionally. She believes in His power, but doesn't fully believe he will show up for her. She says she have faith, but still live as if she must do everything alone. Avoidance doesn't just distance her from people. It distances her from divine support.

But transformation begins the moment she realizes that what she calls strength is actually self-protection, and what she calls independence is fear dressed up as capability. When she begins to soften intentionally, gently, and courageously, she opens the door for her next level to finally reach her. She learns that letting love in is not a threat.

When the avoidant woman heals, she becomes unstoppable. Not because she suddenly becomes emotional, but because she learns the sacred balance between independence and intimacy. She allows God to be the author of her journey, and people to support her. She becomes receptive and open. And for the first time in her life, she becomes fully available for the next level that has been waiting for her all along.

— HOW THE DISMISSIVE AVOIDANT WOMAN SHOWS UP IN EVERYDAY LIFE

The avoidant woman moves through everyday life appearing calm, composed, and in control, but beneath that exterior is a heart shaped by old wounds she rarely speaks about. She often feels suffocated when someone wants too much of her time or attention, because closeness awakens fears she learned to suppress. Questions about her emotions make her uncomfortable. Not because she lacks feeling, but because expressing those feelings once led to disappointment, and judgement. When conflict arises, she retreats inward or withdraws entirely. She choosing silence over vulnerability, and distance over the risk of being emotionally exposed. She prefers texting rather than deep conversations, because digital space gives her room to breathe without the pressure of emotional sensitivity. After a moment of intimacy, emotional or physical, she instinctively pulls back, creating space to regain the control her nervous system believes is necessary for survival.

She often immerses herself in work, projects, or hobbies. Not just out of passion, but because productivity feels safer than emotional connection. She avoids depending on others because she learned early that depending led to disappointment or inconsistency. As soon as her emotions begin to deepen, she may unconsciously sabotage the connection by withdrawing, nitpicking flaws, or convincing herself she's "not ready" or "not interested." She is the woman who says, "I don't care," even when her heart aches with the weight of everything she never learned how to say. She is the woman who walks away first. Not out of pride, but out of fear that being left would hurt far more. She is the woman who prides herself on being unbothered, because being bothered feels dangerously vulnerable. She carries herself with self-assurance, but inside she holds quiet cravings for depth, intimacy, and emotional safety that she struggles to admit; even to herself.

Behind her calm exterior lives a heart that hopes someone will one day approach her gently, patiently, consistently enough for her walls to soften. And until she heals, she will continue showing up in ways that protects her heart. Even when those same protections keep her from the love and connection she secretly yearns for.

—— SHE SHRINKS HER EMOTIONAL NEEDS TO FEEL IN CONTROL

The avoidant woman doesn't simply withdraw from others, she shrinks her emotional needs to feel safe and in control. Where the anxious woman shrinks to stay accepted, the avoidant woman shrinks to stay protected. She convinces herself that she is better off alone. That needing someone is a liability, and emotions are distractions. She believes that closeness only complicates life. She reassures herself that independence is the highest form of strength, because depending on someone once led to emotional neglect. So she builds her life around autonomy. Not because she truly desires isolation, but because isolation once felt like the only place she could avoid pain.

Over time, her self-sufficiency becomes excessive. She takes pride in handling everything, solving everything, managing everything, and consulting no one. She becomes so accustomed to meeting her own needs that she stops allowing anyone else to contribute meaningfully to her world. She struggles to ask for help, not because she doesn't need it, but because needing someone feels like surrendering the emotional control that helped her survive childhood. She becomes the woman everyone relies on but who relies on no one. The woman who appears strong but carries silent emotional exhaustion. The woman who supports others effortlessly but doesn't know how to let others support her.

Her emotional self-sufficiency becomes a shield. One that protects her from disappointment but also blocks her from intimacy. She can manage life, but she cannot fully experience it. She can maintain relationships, but she cannot fully enter them. It's possible for her to love deeply, but she is unable to fully show it. She can crave connection, but doesn't have the capacity fully receive it.

And this is where avoidance sabotages manifestation.

— HER HEARTBREAK ISN'T FROM INTIMACY; IT'S FROM EMOTIONAL STARVATION

Avoidant women rarely have their hearts broken by lovers. Instead, their hearts quietly break from the love they never allow themselves to receive. She longs for deep connection, yet she blocks it before it can reach her. She desires partnership, but she unconsciously sabotages it the moment it begins to feels real. She wants closeness, but she retreats the moment vulnerability is required. She yearns to be understood, but rarely speaks her truth aloud. She craves intimacy, but she chooses control because control feels safer than emotional exposure. Her heartbreak isn't rooted in what others have done to her. It's rooted in all the love she has kept herself from experiencing.

This kind of heartbreak is quiet but devastating. It is the ache of emotional hunger. The hunger for connection, for belonging, being deeply known, while simultaneously keeping the door closed to those very experiences. It is the loneliness of never being truly seen, not because no one tried, but because she never let them in. It is the internal grief of knowing she wants more but feeling paralyzed by the fear of what "more" might cost her. She convinces herself she is fine, she is strong, she is independent, and she doesn't need much. But the truth is, her spirit is starving for emotional nourishment her childhood taught her she was not allowed to receive.

And this emotional starvation becomes a major barrier to her manifestations. Manifestation thrives in openness. The openness to receive love, opportunity, support, guidance, and abundance. But avoidance thrives in restrictions by staying closed, controlled, guarded, and distant.

She cannot step into her highest self while refusing to let anyone see the fullness of who she truly is. Intimacy requires her heart to be open enough to receive what she has prayed for. But avoidance keeps her living behind a shield, watching blessings approach only to convince herself she doesn't need them. She cannot call in intimate, soul-aligned relationships while hiding behind emotional walls. She will elevate into her next level when she unlocks her heart and remove the layers of old survival patterns.

The truth is simple but profound: her heartbreak is not from the world. It is from the distance she maintains from the very love, connection, and intimacy she was designed to experience. And healing begins the moment she gives herself permission to soften, to open, to be seen, and to receive the kind of emotional nourishment her spirit has been starving for all along.

⎯⎯ THE TURNING POINT: WHEN DISMISSIVE AVOIDANT WOMEN BEGIN TO AWAKEN

The turning point for an avoidant woman arrives the moment she begins to awaken to the truth of her own heart. For so long, she believed her independence was her identity. That doing everything alone made her strong, capable, and untouchable. But awakening reveals that her independence was a shield, not her nature. It was the armor she had to wear, not the essence of who she truly is. She begins to understand that her emotional distance was protection, not preference. That her detachment was a survival mechanism, not a reflection of her heart. Her avoidance was rooted in fear, not freedom. Self-reliance was a necessity created by childhood, not a divine design for adulthood. This realization shakes her deeply, but it also frees her.

As she awakens, she learns that needing love does not weaken her, it humanizes her. Wanting connection does not make her fragile, it makes her whole.

It requires allowing people to meet you emotionally without assuming they will disappoint you. Challenging the belief that emotional independence is strength, and embracing the truth that healthy interdependence; the balance of connection and autonomy, is real power. It means learning to trust that closeness doesn't always lead to loss and intimacy doesn't always end in pain, It's her coming into the realization that being seen doesn't mean being judged.

CHAPTER 7

Fearful Avoidant/ Disorganized Attachment

CHAPTER 7

FEARFUL AVOIDANT/ DISORGANIZED ATTACHMENT

 Disorganized attachment is the most complex style because it is rooted in confusion. A woman with this style often experienced relationships where love and fear coexisted. Caregivers may have been inconsistent; safe at times and unsafe at others. As a result, she learned to crave connection while simultaneously fearing it.

Disorganized attachment creates internal contradictions. She wants closeness but fears intimacy. There is a desire for stability, but feels unsettled when she has it. She may push someone away one moment and cling to them the next. Love becomes a dance of pursuit and retreat, longing and avoidance, hope and fear.

This attachment style creates emotional chaos that interferes with manifestation. She expects instability, and her nervous system feels more comfortable in chaos than in peace. Attracting unpredictable relationships is comfortable, because they matches her internal state. She craves love, but question its sincerity. Desires growth, but fear what change might require.

Breaking free involves creating internal safety where none existed. She has to teach her nervous system that peace is not a trap. She must learn consistency, not just with others but within yourself. It is imperative to choose partners who value stability rather than those who mirrors your past.

Manifest Me guides the disorganized woman toward harmony, and inner alignment so she can finally receive the love and life she deserves. Disorganized attachment creates a world where love feels like both the safest place and the most dangerous one. It is the emotional contradiction that forms when a woman grows up in environments marked by instability, unpredictability, emotional chaos, or trauma. Childhood becomes a place where comfort and fear are intertwined. Where the person she needs for safety is also the source of her anxiety, confusion, or hurt.

She learns to love in the midst of instability long before she has the language to understand what she is absorbing. It was modeled to attach in an atmosphere filled with emotional mixed signals; warmth one moment, withdrawal the next. She learns to bond through fear, confusion, and unpredictability. Unfortunately, closeness and pain shown in the same breath. Her developing nervous system becomes trained to associate love with emotional turbulence, affection with inconsistency, and connection with uncertainty. The very people meant to make her feel safe, became the same people who create internal chaos, leaving her without a clear distinction between comfort and danger, nurture and neglect, love and fear.

As she grows into a woman, these early emotional lessons follow her. She moves through love with an internal tug-of-war. Wanting closeness desperately but fearing it just as deeply. Her heart reaches while her nervous system retreats. She becomes the woman who craves intimacy but fears exposure, who opens her heart one moment and shuts down the next, who loves intensely but trusts reluctantly. She desires connection, yet she anticipates pain. She longs to be held, yet she prepares to be hurt. She wants to be chosen, yet she expects to be abandoned. Her spirit desires partnership, yet her body remembers instability.

To her, love feels like a battlefield. Not because she seeks conflict, but because love was never peaceful in her earliest memories. Affection came with tension, while proximity came with unpredictability. Any type of attachment was an emotional risk. So in adulthood, her heart does not rest easily. She is constantly navigating between desire and fear, closeness and distance, longing and self-protection. Love does not automatically feel safe. It feels like something she has to survive.

And until she heals the emotional blueprint she inherited, she will continue mistaking instability for passion, anxiety for connection, and emotional unpredictability for love. This is not her fault, but once she becomes aware, she gains the power to transform it.

— SHE LIVES IN EMOTIONAL CONTRADICTION

A fearful/disorganized woman is not confused because she lacks clarity, she is confused because her earliest experiences with love were unpredictable, inconsistent, and emotionally contradictory. She learned that closeness comes with risk, that affection comes with tension, and that safety can shift without warning. In childhood, the people who were supposed to protect her were also the ones who frightened her, overwhelmed her, or failed to show up in ways that made her feel secure. So she internalized the belief that love is unstable, that attachment is dangerous, and that the very thing she desires may also be the thing that hurts her.

Her childhood may have whispered mixed emotional messages: "I love you… but I'm overwhelmed by you." "Come close… but not too close." "I need you… but I can't show up for you." "You matter… but I'm inconsistent." "You can trust me… but not fully." These contradictions didn't just shape how she felt about relationships, they trained her nervous system to stay in survival mode. Constantly scanning for shifts, changes, and emotional storms. She learned that affection can quickly turn into rejection, and trust can dissolve without explanation.

As an adult, she carries these emotional imprints into every connection. She wants the warmth of love, but fears losing control. She craves emotional support, but fears becoming dependent on someone who may not be there when she needs them most. She longs for security, but expects unpredictability because predictability never existed for her. To others, it appears as though she is conflicted, but the truth is deeper: her heart longs for connection, but her nervous system expects harm. Her emotions pull her toward closeness while her trauma pulls her toward distance. Love feels like both a sanctuary and a threat.

Her heart is not confused. Her nervous system is dysregulated. It is responding to past danger, not present reality.

It is because her earliest emotional environment taught her that the people she relied on could also hurt her, abandon her, or overwhelm her without warning. This is the internal war of the disorganized woman. The longing for love against the fear of it, the desire for closeness against the instinct to flee, and the craving for emotional security against the expectation of emotional chaos. But once she begins to understand the origin of these patterns, she opens the door to healing. Not by rejecting connection, but by slowly learning that safety can exist, consistency is possible, and love does not have to feel unpredictable.

— SHE PROTECTS HERSELF BY BECOMING BOTH ANXIOUS AND AVOIDANT

A woman with disorganized attachment protects herself by being both anxious and avoidant, often in the same relationship and sometimes in the same moment. Disorganized attachment is not a single pattern. It is two emotional worlds battling for dominance inside her. When she fears abandonment, her anxious side emerges. She clings tightly to the people she loves, seeking reassurance, craving closeness, panicking at emotional distance, and trying to hold the relationship together with all her strength. She becomes hyper-aware of shifts in tone, space, or energy, because her nervous system has been trained to expect people to disappear without warning. But when she fears intimacy, when closeness starts to feel overwhelming, suffocating, or unpredictable, her avoidant side surfaces. She shuts down emotionally. She retreats inward. She distances herself. She becomes quiet, withdrawn, unreachable, and self-contained again. For her, connection and danger have always been tangled together, so even when she wants love desperately, she cannot trust it fully.

She becomes the woman who silently pleads, "Don't leave me," while simultaneously whispering internally, "Don't get too close." Both closeness and distance trigger her because both were emotionally unsafe in her past. She longs for connection but braces for betrayal. She desires intimacy but prepares for instability. She wants partnership but expects chaos. This internal tug-of-war is not her being dramatic, unstable, or complicated. It is her trying to navigate relationships with a nervous system that never learned what stability feels like. Her emotional world has two voices speaking at once: one terrified of being alone, the other terrified of being vulnerable.

Her behaviors are not contradictions, they are trauma responses. She may cling when she feels ignored and withdraw when she feels exposed. She chases partners who pull away and push away partners who move towards her. She can feel deeply connected one moment and suddenly overwhelmed the next. She wants love with her heart, but distrusts it with her body. Her spirit desires intimacy, but her nervous system reacts as if love itself is a threat. The push-pull dynamic that confuses others is the only emotional language she learned in environments where comfort and chaos arrived in the same arms.

Deep down, she is not difficult. She is dysregulated. She is not confused about what she wants, she is confused about what feels safe. It may appear indecisive, but she is just trying to reconcile two emotional truths that have never lived in peace within her. And while her patterns may feel exhausting, they make perfect sense when understood through the lens of her upbringing. A heart raised in contradiction, becomes a heart that struggles to trust its own desires.

Yet this awareness is the beginning of liberation. Once she recognizes that her reactions are rooted in emotional memory rather than current reality, she can begin the work of creating safety within herself. Something she never received consistently as a child. And slowly, she learns that she does not have to live forever in the emotional chaos she inherited. She can become a woman who no longer fears her own vulnerability, confuses instability with connection, and no longer battles herself in love. This is where her healing and her true becoming begins.

— HER NERVOUS SYSTEM LIVES IN HYPERVIGILANCE

The fearful/disorganized woman lives with a nervous system caught in perpetual hypervigilance. Unlike the anxious woman who fears being left, and the avoidant woman who fears being truly seen, the disorganized woman fears both simultaneously. Her body is wired for contradiction. Her heart wants closeness, but her nervous system prepares for threat. Her mind desires connection, but her instincts anticipate danger. She is always scanning, not because she is paranoid, but because her earliest emotional lessons taught her that stability is temporary and safety is fragile.

She is always bracing for the "shift,"; the emotional change, the withdrawal, the explosion, the silence, or the disappointment she once endured without warning. Her body has become conditioned to expect the worst, not because she is dramatic, but because instability was once her only emotional language.

Her nervous system never rests. Even in healthy relationships, she anticipates chaos. She can have a stable partner, but she still waits for abandonment. Even when she is safe, she searches for signs of danger. It is not intentional. It is instinctual. Her body remembers the times when love turned into fear, affection turned into discomfort, and protection turned into unpredictability. So she enters every relationship half-present and half-prepared for loss. Her body speeds up at the possibility of closeness and tightens at the possibility of separation. Joy feels suspicious, and good news feels fragile. She constantly wonders, "How long will this last?" even when nothing is wrong.

This hypervigilance becomes exhausting. Her spirit wants rest, but her nervous system remains alert. She becomes a woman living in emotional duality. She's longing for connection while preparing for it to collapse. To her, love does not feel like a place to land; it feels like a place to monitor. And because her earliest experiences taught her that the people she depended on could also harm her, she never fully settles, even with healthy partners, stable friendships, or supportive environments.

Her hypervigilance is not a flaw. It is a survival strategy her younger self created to emotionally navigate unpredictability. But what once kept her safe now keeps her stuck. Healing begins not by judging this pattern, but by understanding it. When she starts to separate memory from the present moment, her nervous system can slowly learn to rest. She can begin to feel safe in stillness, secure in connection, and grounded in love without waiting for it to break. And this shift from hypervigilance to inner safety. It becomes the foundation for her emotional freedom and spiritual becoming.

— HOW SHE SHOWS UP IN EVERYDAY LIFE

The fearful or disorganized woman moves through everyday life with an emotional world that feels contradictory even to herself. She feels uncomfortable when someone becomes distant because distance awakens her fear of abandonment, yet she feels overwhelmed when someone gets too close because closeness awakens her fear of being hurt. The fearful avoidant becomes clingy during moments of insecurity, reaching for reassurance and connection, but then becomes cold or distant during moments of vulnerability, retreating to protect herself from the very intimacy she craves. She opens up quickly, often sharing deeply and intensely, because she longs to be understood, but then shuts down just as fast, because her nervous system panics at the idea of being seen too clearly. She may express her deepest emotions one day and disappear the next. Not because she is manipulative or inconsistent, but because connection activates both her longing and her fear. She spends her relationships testing people. Reaching out to see if they will stay, pushing them away to see if they will return, because predictability was not a part of her emotional childhood.

She often over-reacts to perceived threats, like a tone change, a delayed response, or emotional distance, because her nervous system is trained to anticipate instability. Yet she under-reacts to genuine harm or unhealthy patterns because emotional chaos feels normal to her. She becomes drawn to emotionally unavailable, unpredictable, or inconsistent partners because chaos is familiar and familiarity feels safe, even when it is painful. At the same time, she struggles to trust good people, stable partners, and peaceful relationships because goodness feels foreign. Safety feels suspicious. Consistency feels emotionally strange. Her nervous system mistakes peace for boredom, healthy love for danger, and stability for an illusion that could shatter at any moment. She finds comfort in instability, not because she desires dysfunction, but because her earliest experiences conditioned her to associate love with unpredictability.

The disorganized woman is not broken, and she is not dramatic. She is not "too much" or "hard to love." She is a woman trying to regulate an emotional system that was never regulated for her. She learned to live in emotional contradictions because her environment taught her contradictory lessons.

As a result, she enters adulthood with a nervous system that does not know the difference between safety and danger. Every relationship becomes a battlefield between the part of her that craves connection and the part that fears it.

Her behaviors; the push, the pull, the cling, and the retreat, are not personality flaws. They are the survival patterns of a woman who learned to protect herself in emotionally unpredictable environments. And beneath those patterns is a heart that desperately wants to feel safe, loved, and understood. Once she learns to regulate her inner world, her patterns begin to make sense, her reactions soften, and her spirit becomes capable of receiving the kind of love and stability she has always deserved.

In everyday life, the disorganized woman often experiences emotional whiplash within herself. She may wake up feeling close and connected to someone, but by midday she feels detached, irritable, or unsure why she suddenly wants space. She may reread conversations, not because she doubts the other person, but because her own feelings shift so rapidly, she struggles to trust them. She starts projects with enthusiasm but abandons them when the emotional intensity becomes overwhelming. She can be warm and deeply loving in one moment, then guarded and distant the next. Leaving even herself confused by her own reactions. Simple stressors can trigger old emotional memories, making her withdraw without explanation. She often feels like she is managing both a longing for closeness and a fear of it throughout her daily routine, making even ordinary interactions feel heavier than they should.

She also tends to misinterpret neutral situations through a lens shaped by old instability. When someone takes a while to respond, she may assume rejection or anger. When someone expresses care or compliments her, she questions their intentions. When plans are uncertain, she experiences anxiety, but when plans are consistent, she feels pressure. She becomes hyper-aware of tone changes, body language, and energy shifts. Her nervous system responds to everyday moments as if they are emotional emergencies, even when nothing threatening is happening. As a result, she may isolate when she actually needs comfort, or she may seek reassurance when she actually needs space. She may resist help because receiving care feels unfamiliar, yet she feels hurt when no one steps in.

Her daily life becomes a series of emotional negotiations between the part of her that wants to be loved and the part of her that fears what love might cost.

— HOW FEARFUL AVOIDANT/DISORGANIZED ATTACHMENT BLOCKS HER FROM MANIFESTING

A disorganized woman blocks herself from manifesting what she truly desires because her internal world is constantly conflicted. She longs for stability but is conditioned to expect chaos, so when something stable arrives; a healthy partner, a peaceful opportunity, a consistent environment, she questions it, mistrusts it, or pushes it away.

Manifest Me requires clarity, but she lives in emotional confusion. She cannot name what she wants without simultaneously fearing it. Her desires feel dangerous because in her earliest experiences, So even when she prays for alignment, her nervous system prepares for abandonment. When she visualizes abundance, her body anticipates loss. Even when she feels called to move rise, her emotions pull her backward into survival mode.

She blocks what she wants because her nervous system treats her desires as threats. She wants connection, but the moment it becomes real, she shuts down or retreats to avoid the vulnerability required to receive it. She seeks to be successful, but as soon as opportunities grow, she self-sabotages. Fearing the responsibility, exposure, or pressure that success brings, causes her to stand still. She sets her heart for emotional peace, but she gravitates toward chaotic environments or unpredictable people, because chaos feels familiar and familiarity feels safe. She longs for consistency, but will put it to the test until it breaks. When she experiences intimacy, she mistrusts it until it feels distant again. She decides to move forward, but is constantly pulled backward by old emotional reflexes that whisper, "Something is about to go wrong."

Her manifestations become blocked because her nervous system is manifesting from fear while her spirit is manifesting from desire. She cannot hold what she calls in because she is subconsciously prepared to lose it. It's difficult to receive blessings when receiving requires openness, and openness feels unsafe.

Trusting is out of the question, to what is aligned when she has only ever known instability. Instead of aligning with what she wants, she aligns with what she remembers. All she know is inconsistency, confusion, and emotional unpredictability. The result is a life built from childhood programming instead of adult individuality.

This is why she feels stuck, frustrated, and confused. She is praying for one thing while her nervous system is protecting her from the very thing she is praying for. Until she heals, the emotional contradictions within her, will continue to block the stability, and abundance she deeply longs for. But once she learns to regulate her emotions, rebuild her internal sense of safety, and separate the past from the present, she changes to being open to manifest from a spirit of expectation instead of the spirit of fear. And when she does, everything she once ran from, shifts to everything she is finally able to receive.

—— SHE SHRINKS NOT OUT OF FEAR; BUT OUT OF CONFUSION

While the anxious woman shrinks to stay accepted and the avoidant woman shrinks to stay protected, the disorganized woman shrinks because she has never learned whether love is a place to run toward or a place to run from. Her entire emotional world feels contradictory, so she often feels lost inside her own reactions. One moment her heart reaches out, craving connection with genuine intensity. The next moment her nervous system panics, telling her the same connection is unsafe. She does not trust her emotions because they shift rapidly. She cannot always trust others because stability feels suspicious; almost too good to be true. She struggles to trust peace because peace feels unfamiliar, even uncomfortable, compared to the emotional chaos she grew up navigating.

Her shrinking has nothing to do with weakness or lack of worth. It is rooted in the lack of internal safety she experienced in her earliest attachments. When safety was unpredictable in childhood, emotional inconsistency became her normal. So as an adult, the absence of chaos feels threatening. The presence of vulnerability feels risky, and the experience of love feels confusing. She pulls back not because she wants to disappear, but because she genuinely cannot tell whether intimacy will nurture her or harm her. Her inner world has been trained to brace for impact even during moments of tenderness.

She is torn between two emotional truths that both feel so real. The truth that says, "I want to be loved," and the truth that says, "Love is dangerous." Her nervous system is pulled in opposite directions. One part of her wanting to run toward love and the other part wanting to run away from it. This creates an emotional tension that leaves her exhausted, confused, and unable to fully anchor into the life she longs for.

The heartbreaking reality is that she often blames herself for this confusion. She may believe she is "too much," "unstable," "hard to love," or "broken," when in fact, she is simply a woman who had to learn how to navigate attachment without the consistency every child deserves. Her nervous system is not malfunctioning. It is doing exactly what it was trained to do in order to survive unpredictable emotional environments. And because her sense of safety was never regulated in childhood, she enters adulthood with an emotional compass that swings back and forth, making it difficult to discern whether vulnerability is a doorway to connection or a doorway to pain.

This emotional whiplash blocks manifestation in profound ways. Manifestation requires certainty and stability, but she lives in internal conflict. In order to manifest, clarity is needed, but she has lived a lifetime of mixed signals. Manifestation demands trust. Trust in herself, others, and in God. She must be able to trust in the process. This becomes a difficult task, because trust was the very foundation that was compromised in her earliest relationships.

Her heartbreak is not failure. It is a story of emotional resilience. It is the story of a woman who learned to love without a map. She was made to survive without stability, and to navigate connection without a model for safety. But when she begins to heal, when she begins to regulate, and rebuild her internal world, she becomes capable of receiving love in ways that finally match the depth of what she has always desired.

THE TURNING POINT: WHEN FEARFUL AVOIDANT-DISORGANIZED WOMAN BEGIN TO AWAKEN

The turning point for the disorganized woman arrives the moment she realizes that nothing about her emotional world is random, broken, or shameful. Her intensity is not a flaw, but a natural response to a childhood where emotional stability was inconsistent. Her fear is not irrational. It is memory stored in her nervous system. Her confusion is not weakness, however it is the inevitable result of being taught to associate love with both comfort and danger. Her triggers are not signs of immaturity. They are echoes of needs that were never met, soothed, or understood. Her patterns are not character defects. They are survival strategies her younger self created to navigate unpredictable emotional terrain. And when she finally understands that every reaction she has ever had was learned, she gains the sacred permission to unlearn what no longer serves her.

This awakening is profound. When she recognizes that her fear was inherited, not chosen, she stops blaming herself and begins to build new emotional pathways rooted in safety rather than panic. In the event she accepts that chaos, inconsistency, and instability were once her emotional teachers, she stops judging her adult self for the blueprint she was given. Considering that true safety was never modeled for her, she stops feeling defective for struggling and begins the powerful work of creating safety within herself. For the first time, she realizes she is not broken; she is whole.

Her transformation accelerates when she stops fighting her emotional contradictions and begins nurturing the parts of herself that were never affirmed. She doesn't see her reactions as problems, she sees them as parts of her that are asking for healing. Instead of trying to silence her fears, she begins listening to what they are trying to protect. Rather than hiding her sensitivity, she honors it as the doorway to her intuition. As she tends to the inner child who survived instability, she's now a woman capable of manifesting from inner peace.

She learns emotional regulation; the ability to calm her nervous system without collapsing her world.

She builds a secure connection with herself; honoring her needs, her emotions, and her truth. She is unshakeable. This is the moment she is grounded, centered, and emotionally anchored. And in this new state, she becomes powerful in a way she has never known before.

She becomes the woman she was always meant to be. Not shaped by chaos, but shaped by healing. A woman whose identity is rooted in safety, not fear. She emerges into a woman who trusts her emotional compass. She welcomes love without bracing for loss. A woman who manifests from clarity, intention, and inner strength. She no longer runs from herself, but returns home to herself. This awakening marks the beginning of her most powerful transformation yet.

CHAPTER 8

Secure Attachment

CHAPTER 8

SECURE ATTACHMENT

 The woman who can finally manifest herself fully is not perfect. She is emotionally safe. Secure attachment is not about flawless relationships, behaviors, or pasts. It is about learning to trust yourself enough to show up with clarity. Becoming securely attached begins with seeing your patterns clearly and choosing to respond differently. It requires taking responsibility for your emotional world, regulating your internal reactions, and building an unshakeable sense of trust within yourself. A secure woman knows how to advocate for her needs without fear. She holds boundaries without guilt. She communicates openly and honestly. She trusts her intuition with confidence, and sees connection as something to be experienced, not something to fear. Secure attachment is not something you stumble into. It is something you consciously practice. Every time you choose truth over fear, boundaries over people-pleasing, honesty over silence, stability over chaos, and identity over insecurity, you move one step closer to becoming the secure woman you were always meant to be.

A secure woman manifests her highest self with ease because she is no longer fighting an internal war. Her mind, body, and spirit moves in agreement. She trusts herself, decisions, and her resilience. She welcomes love into her life, and understand it belongs there. There is no need to chase connections, because she attracts it. She doesn't shrink to make others comfortable, she expands. A secure woman releases what hurts with grace. She steps into the next level boldly, knowing she is built for it. Secure attachment becomes the soil where Manifest Me grows, because a woman rooted in emotional safety cannot be shaken by external instability.

Secure attachment is the emotional home every woman deserves. Not the home she may have come from, but the home she builds within herself. It is not perfection, flawlessness, or a life without pain. It is emotional steadiness and inner grounding. The deep knowing that you can trust yourself to navigate life with clarity and strength. A securely attached woman does not operate from fear; she lives, moves, and have her being from truth. She does not respond from old wounds, because she secure within herself. It is not in her to react from panic, because she responds from composure.

She is not without triggers. She just does not allow triggers to dictate her life. She is not without insecurities, but she does not let insecurities narrate her story. She experiences pain in her life, but she knows pain is not her personality. Secure attachment is not the absence of adversity. It is the presence of inner safety, and from this safety, she manifests the life she was always destined to live.

— SHE MOVES THROUGH THE WORLD WITH EMOTIONAL STABILITY

A securely attached woman moves through the world with an inner steadiness that cannot be shaken by external shifts. She has learned either through nurturing or through deep emotional healing that she is safe within herself. Her intuition is no longer drowned out by fear. Her voice is not silenced by doubt. Her decisions are no longer hijacked by old trauma. She trusts her own heart, judgment, and ability to navigate life with confidence. Where the anxious woman chases reassurance, the avoidant woman rejects vulnerability, and the disorganized woman fears both closeness and distance, the secure woman understands that connection is not something to cling to, fear, or run from. Connection becomes something she holds with openness. Understanding it is not what she must sacrifice herself to maintain, but to nurture as an asset in her life.

She does not crumble when someone pulls away because she knows distance is not always dangerous. When someone sets boundaries, there is no need to implode, because she recognizes boundaries as an act of love, not rejection.

She does not betray herself to preserve a relationship because she understands that any connection requiring the abandonment of her authenticity is not a connection aligned with her spirit. Her worth is not tied to someone else's emotional availability, validation, or consistency. She refrains from interpreting another person's limitations as a reflection of her value. She knows that someone's inability to show up fully has nothing to do with her worthiness and everything to do with their own internal landscape.

A securely attached woman does not fear being alone, because her solitude is peaceful and purposeful. She does not view relationships as a place of threat but as a place of expansion, learning, and connection. She welcomes love without chasing it, receives affection without questioning it, and expresses her needs without apologizing for them. Her emotional world is not ruled by survival. It is ruled by wisdom. And because she operates from emotional stability, she attracts relationships, opportunities, and environments that matches her solid foundation.

Her stability is not coldness. It is clarity and discernment. She has mastered the art of being anchored in herself, and because of that, her presence feels soothing, steady, and spiritually secure. This is the woman who manifests effortlessly, loves intentionally, and rises unapologetically. Not because life is void of challenges, but because she is no longer fighting battles within herself.

— SHE TRUSTS HERSELF FULLY

A secure woman trusts herself so deeply that her inner world becomes her greatest source of stability. She doesn't have a need to look outward for validation, direction, or confirmation, because she has learned to honor the voice within her. She assured of her decisions, because she makes them from clarity rather than survival. Her standards are rooted in worth and not wounds. She trusts her boundaries because she understands they are expressions of self-respect, not barriers to love. And she trusts her ability to walk away from anything or anyone that disturbs her peace, lowers her value, or misaligns with her identity.

This level of self-trust is not arrogance, but it is spiritual alignment and emotional maturity.

She knows that choosing herself is not selfish. It is sacred stewardship over her soul. She recognizes that prioritizing her peace is not avoidance. It is wisdom, an acknowledgement that her nervous system thrives in calmness, not chaos. She understands that honoring her needs is not an inconvenience. It is a responsibility and commitment to never abandon herself. Her self-trust becomes the emotional grounding that stabilizes her through uncertainty. It becomes the internal foundation that prevents her from collapsing under pressure or seeking external reassurance to feel whole. Peace becomes her baseline, a natural state rather than a temporary escape. Confidence is her quiet strength, not loud and performative, but deeply rooted and unwavering. Clarity acts as her compass, guiding her choices, relationships, purpose, and her paths.

Because she trusts herself, there is no question whether she is worthy of love, success, respect, or abundance. She expects it. There is no need to over-explain herself because she knows her intentions are pure. She does not overextend herself, because she understands that self-neglect creates spiritual imbalance. She won't stay in misaligned spaces, because she knows confusion is God's way of saying, "This is not for you." Her self-trust allows her to stand firm in seasons of uncertainty without spiraling, to face challenges without losing her center, and to make aligned choices without fear of judgment.

Her self-trust transforms how she moves through relationships. She doesn't fear being alone, because she is aware that aloneness is not emptiness. It is intimacy with herself. She won't settle for breadcrumbs, because she knows love should nourish, not deplete. Tolerating inconsistency disrupts her peace, so she releases herself from it without guilt.

Her emotional world is steady, and her presence is anchored because she trusts that she can handle whatever life brings with grace. In this state, her manifestations flow easily because she is not blocking them with doubt, fear, or self-betrayal. She trusts that what is meant for her cannot miss her. She is equipped for her next level because she trusts herself fully. She is a woman who moves with certainty, receives with openness, and manifests with power.

— SHE COMMUNICATES HER NEEDS WITHOUT FEAR

A secure woman communicates her needs without fear because her worth is not tied to how others react to her truth. She won't silence herself to keep the peace, because she understands that peace built on suppression is not peace. It is self-abandonment. She does not water herself down to avoid conflict, because she understands that conflict handled with honesty and care becomes a doorway to deeper connection. She ceases from shrinking her needs out of fear of being "too much," because she recognizes that the right people will never be threatened by her emotional reality. She realize her needs matter simply because she matters. She knows her feelings are valid, even when others do not understand them.

So she communicates clearly, openly, and respectfully. Not from panic or desperation, but from a grounded sense of self-respect. She can say, "I need more support," without feeling needy. She can say, "I feel disconnected," without feeling dramatic. She can say, "This doesn't align with me," without fearing rejection. She can say, "I'm not comfortable with that," without apologizing. She can say, "I need clarity," without second-guessing herself. She can say, "I deserve reciprocity," because she no longer confuses humility with self-neglect. Her communication is not emotional dumping, but it is emotional honesty. It is the language of a woman who trusts her voice and honors her needs.

To her, boundaries are not battles. They are bridges. They help her create relationships that feel emotionally safe, spiritually aligned, and mutually supportive. Communication is not confrontation. It is a connection. It is how she creates closeness that feels grounded rather than chaotic.

It allows her to remain anchored in who she is, even when navigating difficult conversations. Her relationships thrive because they are rooted in truth, not guessing games. She speaks with clarity and emotional maturity. She understands that love cannot grow in silence, and connection cannot deepen through avoidance. So she speaks; not to control others, but to honor herself. And in doing so, she attracts relationships where communication, validation, and transparency flows naturally, creating a life where emotional safety is the norm, not the exception.

—— SHE CHOOSES A PARTNER WHO REFLECTS HER WHOLENESS

A secure woman chooses a partner who reflects her wholeness because she finally understands that love is meant to support her, not destabilize her. She is drawn to partners who are emotionally steady, communicative, consistent, and safe. Not because she lacks passion, but because she has matured beyond confusion. She will not confuse intensity with intimacy, because she knows intensity often masks instability. She chooses alignment over attachment, reciprocity over one-sided effort, peace over potential, and stability over unpredictability. She refuses to form bonds that require her to abandon herself.

A secure woman is unmoved by inconsistency because inconsistency does not match her internal stability. She is not impressed by emotional games because she has outgrown the need to fight for love. She is not entertained by instability because instability disrupts her peace, and her peace is non-negotiable. She is only available for love that feels like truth. Opens herself up for love that sees her, respects her, and honors her. Healthy love is normal, not because she got lucky, but because she raised her emotional standard.

And the deeper transformation is this: she does not choose a partner from a place of loneliness, longing, or fear. She chooses from fullness and worthiness. Because she doesn't need someone to complete her, but someone who complements her. Her relationships become extensions of her wholeness. She attracts love that expands her, supports her calling, deepens her peace, and honors the woman she is. In her security, she does not lose herself in love; she elevates within it.

—— HOW SHE SHOWS UP IN EVERYDAY LIFE

A securely attached woman shows up in everyday life with a presence that is both grounding and freeing. She influence every space she enters with emotional steadiness. Allowing herself to rest without guilt, she no won't measures her worth by productivity or performance. She asks for help without shame, because she understands that partnership is not weakness; it is wisdom. She receives love without resistance because her heart no longer braces for disappointment.

She shares her feelings without fear of judgment because she trusts her voice and believes in her emotional validity. She lets people be who they are without trying to fix, teach, or rescue them. The secure woman embraces uncertainty without spiraling. Understanding that life unfolds in divine timing. She moves on from relationships without losing herself, because her worth does not depend on who stays or leaves. She sees rejection as redirection. Not a reflection of her inadequacy, but evidence of realignment. She forgives herself without punishment, accepts responsibility without self-blame, and honors her growth without shame.

In the marketplace, she shows up as a leader, even if she's not in a leadership position. She communicates clearly, sets boundaries professionally, and does not allow fear to silence her ideas. She is not intimidated by others, nor does she compete from insecurity. She collaborates from confidence. The secure woman advocates for fair treatment, asks for what she deserves, and walks away from toxic environments without doubting her value. Her presence commands respect because she carries herself with self-respect. She does not overwork to prove herself, nor does she tolerate being undervalued. Her emotional stability makes her reliable, innovative, and solution-oriented. She builds strong professional relationships because she leads from authenticity, not people-pleasing.

With friends, she shows up with consistency, compassion, and honesty. She does not overextend herself to maintain connection, nor does she disappear when things get difficult. She knows how to hold space for others without carrying emotional burdens that are not hers. She celebrates her friends without comparison, supports them without resentment, and sets boundaries without guilt. A secure woman chooses friendships based on alignment, not obligation. She is loyal, but not self-sacrificing. She protects her peace while honoring the peace of those she loves. Her friendships thrive because they are rooted in mutual respect, emotional safety, and truth.

In romantic relationships, she shows up with emotional openness and wisdom. She communicates her needs clearly and listens without defensiveness. A secure woman does not chase, cling, or collapse. She won't shut down, test, or withdraw. She remains grounded whether love is new, deepening, or challenged.

She allows intimacy to unfold without fear, and she addresses conflict without avoidance or panic. The secure woman chooses a partner who reflects her emotional stability, and she offers them the same in return. She loves with softness, strength, safety, and depth, but not performance. She does not settle for half-love because she knows she is worthy of whole love.

In her family, she breaks generational patterns with grace. She does not respond from old wounds or reenact childhood roles. She communicates respectfully while honoring boundaries that protect her emotional health. She does not internalize family guilt or pressure. She forgives, nurtures and love without losing herself. Her presence inspires emotional maturity in others, and she becomes a living example of what growth looks like.

In her spiritual life, she trusts divine timing, embraces alignment, and allows surrender to guide her path. She does not struggle with control. She is open to guidance, receptive to blessings, and anchored in peace. She listens to her intuition, because she knows it is connected to something higher. She walks with God, and listens to his guidance.

In every area of her life, her stability radiates, her peace calms, and her presence is reassuring. She is the woman who can sit in silence without anxiety. She has the ability to speak her truth without trembling, walk away without crumbling, and choose herself without hesitation. Her life becomes a reflection of her inner wholeness, which is steady and deeply rooted in self-worth.

CHAPTER 9

Limerace

CHAPTER 9

LIMERACE

 Limerence is an intense emotional connection that often feels like love but operates more like hunger. It forms when desire attaches itself to fantasy, hope, and emotional need rather than shared reality and mutual presence. Limerence does not grow out of intimacy. It grows out of longing. It feeds on anticipation, uncertainty, and emotional suspense. Which is why it can feel so consuming and so difficult to release.

At the center of limerence is preoccupation. The mind circles around one person, one connection, and one possibility. Thoughts replay conversations and searches for meaning in silence. When there is contact, the body feels relief or excitement. When there is distance, anxiety rises. Peace begins to feel conditional. This is not because the connection is profound, but because the nervous system is activated and searching for regulation through another person.

Limerence often convinces the heart that intensity equals depth. The emotional highs feel spiritual, and the longing feels purposeful. But intensity is not the same as intimacy, and longing is not the same as love. Limerence thrives where clarity is absent. It survives on potential rather than consistency. It keeps the heart oriented toward what could be instead of what actually is.

The emotional impact of limerence is subtle at first and then deeply disruptive. Over time, self awareness begins to erode, and emotional stability becomes dependent on external responses. Limerence is when personal boundaries soften and needs are minimized. It is when red flags are reframed as misunderstandings or timing issues.

The self slowly moves out of the center, and another person becomes the emotional reference point. This is how power quietly shifts away from the individual and into the hands of uncertainty.

Limerence also affects identity. When longing goes unmet or inconsistent, the mind begins to internalize the absence. Worth is questioned and desirability is analyzed. Value feels negotiable. Instead of asking whether the connection is healthy, the focus turns inward toward self-correction and self-blame. Limerence teaches the heart to perform rather than to rest, to wait rather than to choose, and to hope rather than to know.

This pattern is rarely about the person themselves. Limerence usually attaches to emotional wounds that existed long before the connection appeared. It often reflects unmet needs for safety, consistency, reassurance, or belonging. When early attachment experiences were unpredictable or conditional, the nervous system learns to associate love with anxiety. Limerence feels familiar because it mirrors the emotional environment in which connection was first learned.

Because limerence feels so consuming, many women believe the solution is to detach from desire entirely. But healing does not come from shutting down the heart. It comes from regulating it. Overcoming limerence begins with awareness. When the pattern is named, it loses some of its power. The heart begins to separate what is imagined from what is experienced. Fantasy loosens its grip when reality is allowed to speak.

Healing also requires the restoration of self as the primary source of emotional stability. The nervous system must learn that safety does not come from another person's attention. It comes from internal grounding. As emotional regulation strengthens, urgency fades. The need to monitor, interpret, and chase diminishes. Clarity replaces craving, and choice replaces compulsion.

As attachment wounds heal, the pull of limerence softens. The heart becomes less impressed by intensity and more drawn to consistency. Emotional chaos loses its appeal, and peace begins to feel attractive. Love stops feeling like survival and starts feeling like home. What once felt irresistible begins to feel incompatible.

Limerence cannot survive in a grounded woman. It depends on fantasy, emotional hunger, and unresolved longing to stay alive. When emotions are anchored and boundaries are honored, the nervous system settles, and limerence loses its purpose. Nothing needs to be forced away. What is no longer needed simply fades.

Awareness is the beginning of that release. The moment a woman recognizes what limerence truly is; a coping response rather than love, its power weakens. Awareness turns the lights on in places where fantasy once lived unchecked. What was unconscious becomes visible. What was confusing becomes clear. And clarity creates choice.

When Manifest Me is activated, limerence no longer has room to operate. Manifesting identity instead of attachment, dissolves the emotional gaps limerence feeds on. As a woman returns to herself, fills her own cup, and regulates her inner world, the longing that once searched for completion outside of her is met within. The fantasy collapses because reality becomes enough.

The deepest shift happens quietly. The question moves from whether a woman will choose herself to whether she feels safe doing so. In that safety, power returns. Love becomes something she participates in, not something she waits to receive. Desire turns into preference rather than dependency. Connection becomes mutual, steady, and rooted in truth.

This is the movement from limerence to love. From chasing to choosing. From emotional hunger to emotional wholeness. This is where Manifest Me takes root, restoring clarity, grounding identity, and freeing a woman to experience love without losing herself.

CHAPTER 10

The Truth

CHAPTER 10

THE TRUTH

 Attachment reaches far beyond love or romantic connection. It is the emotional framework that shapes the structure of an entire life. It influences self perception, the ability to trust, emotional regulation, and the way the world is interpreted. It quietly becomes the blueprint beneath choices and connections that are permitted to remain.

This is why the highest version of self does not emerge while emotional patterns rooted in fear remain active. Purpose stays out of reach when the heart still anticipates pain. Healthy love struggles to take root when the nervous system is conditioned to recognize chaos as familiar. Abundance remains distant when safety feels unfamiliar to the spirit. Worth stays hidden when full expression feels threatening.

Attachment acts as a gatekeeper because it shapes the lens through which identity is viewed. Expansion is limited by what feels emotionally safe to hold. Receiving is constrained by what the inner world believes is possible. Stepping into the next level requires a foundation no longer anchored in unresolved wounds from the past.

Attachment acts as a gatekeeper because it shapes the lens through which identity is viewed. Expansion is limited by what feels emotionally safe to hold. Receiving is constrained by what the inner world believes is possible. Stepping into the next level requires a foundation no longer anchored in unresolved wounds from the past.

There is more within you than this. A moment comes when awareness opens and you recognize how much of life has been spent showing up for everyone else while neglecting yourself. When carrying burdens never meant to be held alone, and shrinking for the comfort of others while quietly suffocating under expectations.

Reaching the highest expression of self requires freedom from emotional patterns that no longer serve. The heart gravitates toward what is known, even when what is known limits growth. Without healing, the emotional language once used for survival continues to repeat itself.

Healing becomes the doorway. It restores the nervous system, reshapes inner dialogue, resets expectations, and expands the capacity to hold the life that is desired. Healing attachment changes perception of self and the world. Manifest Me represents emotional freedom. Emotional freedom shapes identity. Identity influences behavior, and behavior opens the path to manifestation.

Attachment healing is not a small part of becoming. It is the becoming. It marks the shift from living through wounded survival to living through embodied womanhood. Old emotional patterns rooted in survival are uprooted and replaced with patterns aligned with elevation.

As attachment heals, life begins to align with truth. Love feels safer. Destiny opens in ways once inaccessible. Attachment is not an obstacle but a bridge, it is the initiation, the entryway into the next level. When attachment is healed, a woman becomes able to hold the life designed for her. Healing in this area marks the point where the past releases its grip and the future begins to draw you forward.

This emotional patterning quietly authors your story until awareness teaches you how to take the pen. It influences relationship chapters long before conscious choice appears. Reactions are shaped before logic steps in. Expectations are colored before words are spoken. These patterns function like emotional DNA formed through early experiences, unseen and often unnamed, yet deeply influential.

As healing begins, the work extends beyond connection with others and reaches the inner narrative that has guided an entire life. Childhood agreements start to unravel. This inner framework becomes the gatekeeper because it sets the threshold for receiving. Healing expands capacity, the ability to receive, to rest, to trust, to be visible, to love without self loss, and to rise without fear of falling.

As healing deepens, the nervous system learns a new emotional language rooted in safety rather than survival. Safety becomes the soil where manifestation takes root. With this shift, relationships begin reflecting wholeness. Discernment grows between love and trauma bonding, comfort and familiarity, chemistry and compatibility. Old patterns that once mirrored wounds lose their pull, and choices begin aligning with worth.

Healing in this area opens your awareness, sharpens intuition, fortifies boundaries, and brings clarity to standards. Perception shifts from fear based interpretation to identity rooted discernment. Alignment becomes recognizable without inner struggle. Misalignment is sensed without explanation. Walking away no longer causes collapse, and staying no longer requires self abandonment.

The most powerful change happens within. The future begins to feel believable. Goals feel attainable. Abundance feels natural. Peace becomes sustainable. Confidence settles into consistency. This healing restructures the emotional foundation. Without it, manifestation remains unstable, progress followed by regression, elevation followed by retreat, receiving followed by self sabotage. A thriving life cannot be built on survival based emotional wiring. Once healing occurs, the inner world stops resisting what is being called in and begins preparing for it. What once acted as a gatekeeper becomes a gateway, the bridge between survival and calling.

This work is not optional for the next level. It is the requirement. When the parts shaped by pain, fear, and survival are healed. Access is granted to the woman who has always been there. The next level is not waiting on perfection. It is waiting on a healed emotional foundation. When that foundation shifts, everything built upon it rises as well.

CHAPTER 11

Heal, Align, And Become

CHAPTER 11

HEAL, ALIGN, AND BECOME

 Many women are taught to build their lives from the outside in. The encouragement is to pursue the position, secure the relationship, launch the business, change the environment, and reach the next milestone. For a while, those external shifts feel promising. They bring moments of excitement and a sense of progress.

Yet when the inner world remains unhealed and unaddressed, the same emotional patterns eventually resurface. A new city may offer fresh scenery, but loneliness can still follow. A new relationship may bring hope, but old insecurities often rise again. A new job may feel like a breakthrough, yet self doubt can quietly return. Goals are set with intention, but fear still finds a way to whisper.

This truth is often learned through experience. External change cannot stabilize what is unsettled within. Environment does not override emotional wounds, and new beginnings alone do not erase old beliefs. Lasting transformation begins on the inside. When the inner world is healed, aligned, and strengthened, the outer life naturally follows.

This is why healing is essential, not as punishment or a painful obligation, but as preparation. Healing does not mean a woman is broken. It signals awareness and awakening. It reflects readiness to truly live rather than merely survive. It is the process of aligning life with spirit instead of scars.

Healing also involves releasing outdated versions of self, identities shaped by abandonment, rejection, chaos, or neglect.

Those versions once functioned as protection, offering survival in emotional spaces that lacked safety or guidance. What once acted as armor can later become restrictive, limiting growth and making expansion difficult. When healing begins, space is created to rise freely into a life that reflects wholeness, truth, and purpose.

Healing is a sacred decision to release the version shaped by pain. It is the point where the nervous system finds rest, the battle with imagined threats ends, fear is no longer rehearsed, loss is no longer expected, and emotional weight that never belonged is finally laid down.

Healing becomes a return and a remembering. It reconnects her to the woman she was before shrinking felt necessary and love seemed conditional. Through healing, she reconnects with her true essence.

As the inner world restores, the outer life begins to respond. Cycles driven by fear loose momentum, because fear no longer governs choice. Opportunities are no longer sabotaged, because abundance no longer feels threatening. Connection no longer requires self abandonment, because self trust has been established. Emotional crumbs are no longer accepted, because fullness is understood as a birthright.

Alignment becomes a way of living. Not because challenges disappear, but because self betrayal no longer accompanies difficulty. Healing is not about revisiting the past, but about reshaping the future.
It creates internal safety, making room for external stability. A peaceful life cannot be built while chaos remains unhealed.

Once healing begins, life is built from power rather than panic. Decisions rise to a higher level, and boundaries become firm, and purpose unfolds naturally.

When the inner world is healed, the outer life becomes stable. Healing forms the foundation, and manifestation follows as the result. Healing the inside is not simply one phase along the way. It is the blueprint for the life she is meant to create.

— THE BECOMING PROCESS

Becoming does not arrive in a single moment, decision, or revelation. It unfolds gradually through layers. It is quiet shifts that often go unnoticed until one day it becomes clear that the former version no longer exists. Becoming is a daily return to truth and a consistent commitment to honor the woman the spirit has been waiting to reveal. It is a slow and sacred rising into authenticity.

This process carries both beauty and discomfort, because it requires stretching beyond what feels familiar. Old patterns, fears, roles, and identities may have once felt safe, yet they often acted as silent restraints. Becoming invites expansion into a version that feels at times intimidating. It asks for trust in growth even when the destination is unclear.

Some days feel exhilarating, as though the soul is expanding faster than the body can follow. Other days feel heavy. Grief appears for what is being released. Elevation carries weight because rising always requires letting go. Becoming calls for the release of the version that once ensured survival, lowered standards, and endurance without understanding worth. That version played a role, yet that identity cannot sustain the next level.

Thriving requires more. It is the moment endurance gives way to purpose.

This transition can feel lonely, not because abandonment is happening, but because transformation is taking place. Conversations rooted in scarcity lose their appeal. Environments filled with dysfunction no longer fit. Relationships formed through wounds begin to fade. Roles that demand silence feel restrictive. Identities shaped by fear start to dissolve. This loneliness is not emptiness. It is sacred space.

It is the in between where the former self has released and the emerging self is still forming. It is the pause before elevation, the stretch before movement, the quiet preparation where the spirit readies you for what is next. Growth often feels like isolation because repositioning, recalibration, and redefinition are underway.

This process is not gentle. It is transformative. Old identities are dismantled so new ones can take shape. Comfort is disrupted so purpose can breathe freely. Familiar patterns are challenged so power can rise. Limitations are confronted so greatness can surface. This unfolding is the release of what no longer reflects truth so authenticity can be fully embodied.

Each time the elevated version of self is chosen, boundaries are honored, truth is spoken, intuition is trusted, the past is released, and a deeper step is taken into the life meant for you. Every choice strengthens the foundation and opens access to the next level.

This journey is the intentional surrender into the highest self. It is not a destination, but a path. The journey asks for trust in the unfolding, even when uncertainty is present. It calls for compassion toward who you were while creating space for who you are rising into. It invites belief that growth is worth the discomfort, the transition, the release, the loneliness, and the stretch.

As the journey continues, its beauty becomes clear and growth deepens into transformation. You do more than survive; you rise. Transformation becomes the doorway into a life aligned with your purpose. Every step taken toward yourself moves you closer to your destiny.

── THE ART OF REMEMBERING WHO YOU ARE

There is a version of you that existed long before fear ever found language. A version that moved through life with the freedom only innocence carries. She walked in her essence with confidence because shrinking had not yet been taught.

That version has not disappeared. She has been buried beneath heartbreak, responsibility, survival, and pain. Manifest Me is not about creating someone new. It is about returning to who has always been there. It is not reinvention, but restoration. It is the sacred practice of removing what life placed on you until the truth at your core is revealed again.

Through this return, something powerful begins to unfold. Voice is reclaimed, the one softened to keep peace, avoid tension, remain acceptable, or be chosen. Fire is reawakened, the passion tucked away when strength was demanded over expression. Abandoned dreams resurface after being set aside during heavy seasons. Strength is recognized in places once associated only with pain. Life begins to look less like a record of disappointment and more like proof of resilience.

This remembering changes perception. Self is no longer measured by loss, but by possibility. Identity is no longer shaped by what happened, but by what remains available. In remembering who you are, the future opens with clarity.

Every woman reaches a moment when awareness dawns that she has been living beneath her true power. Something within her stirs and gently whispers that there is more. That realization is not accidental. It is a calling. It is a spiritual awakening signaling that growth has begun and an invitation to return inward. The practice of remembering is the practice of rising. It is a return home to self. It is the reclaiming of power. Once this remembrance takes root, it cannot be undone.

Remembering who you are is an act of reclamation. It is taking back what was lost during seasons of survival. It is choosing truth over narratives formed through pain or circumstance.

It is the shift from seeing yourself through the lens of hurt, to seeing yourself through the lens of purpose. It is the movement from emotional fog into clarity.

As remembrance deepens, tolerance for what diminishes you fades. Spaces that require silence become unbearable. Relationships that drain the spirit loses appeal. Conversations that restrict expansion no longer satisfy. Environments misaligned with growth falls away. Apologies for outgrowing former versions cease because emotional, mental, and spiritual advancement has already occurred.

This remembrance does not create arrogance. It does not make you difficult. It sharpens discernment. It makes you unavailable to anything that contradicts your identity. What once kept you small no longer holds power because the spirit refuses to return to a version already surpassed.

Through remembrance, survival gives way to destiny. Settling is replaced with intention. Validation loses its grip as worth becomes self evident. Light no longer dims because brilliance is finally recognized as the gift it has always been. You stop carrying the identity assigned by wound or circumstance and begin walking in the identity aligned with your purpose.

Every woman experiences a moment. Sometimes subtle, sometimes earth-shattering—where she realizes she has been living beneath her power. A moment where something deep inside awakens and whispers, This is not all of you. You were made for more than this. That moment is not a coincidence; it is calling. It is the spiritual alarm clock signaling that your becoming has begun. It is the divine invitation to return to yourself.

Remembering who you are is a reclamation. It is a taking back of everything the enemy stole from you while you were busy trying to survive. It is the act of choosing truth over the narratives that were placed on you. It is the moment you stop seeing yourself through the eyes of pain and start seeing yourself through the eyes of purpose. It is the work of stepping out of the emotional fog and into the clarity of your identity.

As you remember yourself, you grow less tolerant of anything that diminishes you. You become allergic to spaces that require your silence. You lose interest in relationships that drain your spirit. You outgrow conversations that limit your expansion. You detach from environments that no longer reflect your rising. You stop apologizing for outgrowing what you have already surpassed emotionally, mentally, or spiritually.

Remembering who you are does not make you arrogant. It makes you aligned. It does not make you difficult. It makes you discern. It does not make you unapproachable. It makes you unavailable to anything that contradicts your identity. It becomes impossible to tolerate the things that once kept you small because your spirit refuses to shrink back into a version of yourself you've already transcended.

When you remember who you are, you stop settling for survival and start choosing destiny. You stop bending to fit into places you were meant to evolve out of. You stop chasing validation and realize you are already worthy. You stop dimming your light and realize your brilliance was never the problem. It was the gift. Once you truly remember yourself, forgetting is no longer possible.

— THE RELEASE OF THE OLD SELF

Every true transformation begins with release. Not the kind that happens all at once, but the kind that unfolds gradually and with intention. You cannot step fully into the woman you are growing into while holding tightly to the identity of who you once were. Growth requires room. It calls for clarity. It asks for the loosening of everything that keeps you confined to smallness. That process requires a sacred letting go.

The former version of you is not the enemy. She is the self shaped through pain and uncertainty, formed by what had to be endured, influenced by responsibilities carried for too long, and marked by wounds passed down or absorbed along the way. She emerged in seasons where softness was not an option and choice was not yet visible. She learned how to survive chaos, expect disappointment, quiet her needs, adapt to instability, and make herself smaller because that once felt like protection.

Every true transformation begins with release. Not the kind that happens all at once, but the kind that unfolds in layers and with intention. You cannot step into the woman you are growing into while gripping the identity of who you once were. Growth requires space. It calls for clarity. It asks for a loosening of everything that keeps you tethered to smallness. That process requires a sacred release.

The former version of you is not the enemy. She is the self shaped by pain and uncertainty, formed through survival, molded by responsibility, and influenced by inherited wounds. She emerged in seasons where softness was not available and choice was not yet visible. She learned how to move through chaos. That version served a purpose then, but she is not equipped for where you are headed now.

Letting go begins the moment you stop defending the limits she accepted as normal. It starts when you recognize that fear is not your identity, only an experience you endured. It deepens when you release the need to justify excuses, explain patterns, or grant the past authority over what lies ahead. This release begins the instant you decide, quietly or boldly, to lay down what has been weighing you down.

Releasing the old self is not betrayal. It is liberation.

This release can feel uncomfortable because it asks you to confront the very traits once celebrated as strength. Toughness, emotional numbness, over-functioning, perfectionism, people pleasing, and survival mode, kept life moving even when the spirit was depleted. Releasing these patterns can feel like losing a familiar identity.

To let go of the former self, acknowledgment is required. She carried weight that was never meant to be hers, endured pain that was never deserved, and navigated emotional darkness with little recognition. She preserved life, maintained functionality, and kept momentum. Now it is time for rest.

This release is not harsh. It is gentle and compassionate. It is the sacred moment when the heart speaks to the past self with gratitude and says thank you for getting me here, and now it is safe for me to lead.

As the grip on who you were begins to loosen, space opens for who you are stepping into. Within that space, a subtle yet powerful shift occurs. Lightness begins to surface, not because circumstances immediately change, but because you do. Breathing softens. Thoughts realign. Choices become intentional. Survival no longer feels like home. Emotional emergency mode loses its grip. A deeper understanding emerges that life was never meant to require constant proof of worth.

The release of the old self marks a transition from surviving into truly living.

Letting go is not loss. It is elevation. It is the release of instability to make room for peace, the surrender of scarcity to receive abundance, the laying down of fear to embody confidence. It is the willingness to release versions shaped by trauma so the version shaped by truth can emerge.

What is next cannot take root in old patterns. Expansion does not unfold under the weight of former expectations. Abundance does not thrive beneath the shadow of a past identity. Purpose remains dormant while attachment to what no longer fits is maintained.

Letting go is an act of faith. It is the decision to trust the woman you are growing into more than the version that learned how to survive.

And when the old self is released fully, clarity follows. Peace settles in ways never experienced before.

— THE MAGNETIC WOMAN: WHEN YOU BECOME THE ATTRACTION

A magnetic woman is not created; she is revealed. She does not become magnetic because life finally cooperates or because others finally recognize her worth. She becomes magnetic the moment she sees herself. The moment she decides she is done auditioning for love, validation, or belonging. The moment she stops performing for approval and starts standing firmly in her identity.

She is not a woman who tries to be chosen; she is a woman who chooses herself so fully that everything around her must rise to meet her. Her confidence is not arrogance; it is recognition.

A magnetic woman is not created. She is revealed. Magnetism does not come when life finally cooperates or when others acknowledge her worth. It emerges the moment she truly sees herself. It appears when she decides she is finished auditioning for love, validation, or belonging, and chooses instead to stand firmly.

She does not seek to be chosen. She chooses herself so completely, that everything around her must respond accordingly. Her confidence is not arrogance. It is awareness. She understands her value, recognizes her purpose, and knows that her spirit carries a presence that cannot be duplicated or diminished. She moves with a quiet certainty that says she is enough without needing confirmation.

Her actions are intentional because fear no longer leads her decisions. Truth guides her steps instead of insecurity. Worth is honored through boundaries, discernment, and the way she carries herself into every space. Clarity draws others in. Standards create respect. Peace becomes attractive. Alignment speaks without effort.

Her voice carries calm authority, not because attention is demanded, but because rootedness commands it naturally. Silence is no longer used to maintain harmony, because she understands that her voice is part of her peace.

She does not chase. Her energy speaks for her. Opportunities recognize her because she has become someone who recognizes herself. Love is not begged for, because her presence makes it a privilege. Potential is no longer clung to, because reciprocity is valued. Shrinking no longer feels necessary, because expansion is natural.

True magnetism is not loud or performative. Its power is steady and undeniable. Authenticity radiates without force. There is no need to impress, compete, or prove. Presence speaks first. Spirit fills the room before a word is spoken. Magnetism was never missing. It was buried beneath survival. Fear caused disconnection from inner brilliance, and past relationships planted doubt where certainty once lived.

As healing begins, what was hidden starts to return. Pieces thought to be lost were never stolen, only covered by emotional weight. As the spirit clears what survival required, magnetism reveals itself again, natural, powerful, and unmistakably yours.

As you step into authenticity, your energy begins to shift, and when energy shifts, the world responds. Magnetic women do not attract through effort. They attract through essence. They do not pull others toward them. They illuminate themselves so fully that alignment becomes inevitable. Relationships are not chased. Partners who recognize value are drawn in. Opportunities are not wished for. Calling is embodied, and opportunities respond.

A magnetic woman understands that the outer world reflects inner alignment. Worthiness invites honor. Confidence draws respect. Peace creates stability. Truth aligns with purpose. Joy opens the door to fulfillment. Vision calls destiny forward. This is the power of a woman who has manifested herself first. She does not struggle for a seat at the table. The room adjusts in her presence. She does not force doors open. Doors recognize her and respond.

Magnetism is not about attention. It is about being so deeply connected to yourself that everything meant for you recognizes you without effort.

This is the woman Manifest Me invites you to uncover.

— OVERCOMING SELF- DOUBT AND SELF-SABOTAGE

Self doubt is a quiet thief of destiny. It rarely arrives loudly. Instead, it slips into the mind disguised as caution, humility, or logic. It questions worth in moments meant for confidence. It creates hesitation at doors you were born to walk through. It convinces you that preparation is lacking when capability is already present. Though subtle, its impact is powerful, weakening self trust one thought at a time.

Self sabotage often follows closely behind. It becomes the behavior adopted to avoid the discomfort of expansion. When doubt suggests unreadiness, sabotage finds ways to confirm it. When doubt predicts failure, sabotage creates conditions that lead there. When doubt questions worth, sabotage ensures full effort is never given.

Many women do not sabotage because of inability, but because the nervous system has learned to associate familiarity with safety. Elevation feels unfamiliar. New levels feel unpredictable. Success feels foreign. Love feels risky. Peace feels suspicious. The mind returns to what it recognizes, even when that place is marked by chaos, pain, or limitation.

Self sabotage is not a flaw. It is a learned form of protection. It is the mind saying survival is understood here, but not there. It is the body reacting to change as if danger is present. It is the spirit desiring more while fear resists the unknown. Manifest Me interrupts this cycle by teaching awareness. The obstacle is not weakness, but conditioning that taught you to fear your own greatness.

Doubt does not always look dramatic. It often appears as procrastination, perfectionism, overthinking, or waiting for the perfect moment. It shows up when gifts are minimized, decisions are second guessed, and opportunities once prayed for are declined. It appears every time you believe one more qualification is required before fully stepping into what you already know you are called to do.

Sabotage reveals itself when comfort is chosen the moment growth stretches you. A healthy relationship appears and suspicion follows. An opportunity opens and capability is questioned.

Momentum builds and chaos is introduced to return to familiar ground. The fear is not failure. The fear is elevation, because elevation requires becoming someone unfamiliar.

Manifest Me invites you to face these patterns without shame. Healing requires honesty. Transformation requires acknowledgment. When awareness replaces avoidance, something shifts. Self betrayal ends and self support begins.

Freedom from doubt does not come from silencing fear, but from trusting identity more than insecurity. Truth becomes louder than trauma. Potential begins leading instead of the past. The elevated version of self is chosen even when the familiar one feels easier.

Sabotage loses influence the moment you choose yourself fully and without apology. When shrinking is no longer an option. When dreams are valued enough to endure growth. When faith is chosen over fear. When it becomes clear that the life you desire was never too big, only belief was too small.

Life moves from fear based decisions to identity based living. Choices are made from who you are becoming rather than who you once were. Power is embodied instead of avoided. Voice is declared instead of doubted. Calling is stepped into rather than stepped aside from.

When a woman lives from identity instead of insecurity, sabotage has nothing left to attach itself to. Her rise becomes inevitable.

— REWIRING YOUR MIND AND EMOTIONS

Rewiring your mind goes far beyond changing thoughts. It is the transformation of emotional patterns that have lived within you for years, shaped by survival rather than truth. Every woman carries an inner blueprint formed long before language existed to explain it. The mind learned, the heart adapted, and the nervous system stored what childhood, relationships, and life experiences taught.

When chaos felt normal, the body learned to stay on high alert. When inconsistency was present, the system learned to brace for disappointment.

When affection had to be earned, the spirit learned pursuit instead of reception. The emotional world was trained to expect what was endured, and healing requires teaching it to expect what is deserved.

This work is not simple. It is sacred. It involves showing the mind that safety does not signal danger, allowing the body to experience peace without suspicion, helping emotions understand that joy can last, and reminding the heart that love is not a threat. It asks the nervous system to learn a new rhythm, one grounded in trust rather than fueled by survival.

Rewiring begins with awareness, but it deepens through lived experience. Healing cannot be reasoned into existence. It must be felt. The nervous system responds to repetition, not logic. It learns through consistency, trusting what is returned to again and again, believing what is embodied daily.

As peace becomes familiar, the body relaxes. As stability settles in, the mind stops anticipating collapse. As love feels safe, the heart releases its guard. As worthiness becomes identity, the spirit no longer braces for rejection.

Rewiring is the process of reclaiming authority over your internal world. It is choosing new narratives and supporting them with new behaviors. It is pausing instead of panicking, responding instead of reacting, trusting instead of questioning every decision, and anchoring yourself rather than abandoning yourself emotionally.

This process requires gentleness. Healing does not respond to force or shame. It unfolds through compassion, the same care offered to a child learning safety for the first time. That is exactly what is happening, comforting the inner child who once learned to survive without the security she needed.

As regulation takes place, a shift occurs. Peace begins to feel familiar. Calm registers as safety rather than threat. Emotions settle into order instead of chaos. Self trust grows stronger than fear, stronger than triggers, stronger than echoes of the past.

Rewiring requires gentleness. You cannot bully yourself iHere is where identity transforms, from the inside outward. Manifest Me guides this shift by teaching presence, self soothing, self honoring, and truth speaking. It rebuilds the emotional foundation from survival to security, moving reactions rooted in wounds toward responses grounded in wisdom. Life begins to be experienced from steadiness rather than anxiety.

Rewiring the mind and emotions creates the capacity to hold the life you desire. It forms the bridge between who you were and who you are meant to be. It is the return to emotional safety, self trust, and grounded identity. Once the inner world changes, the outer world follows naturally.

— BOUNDARIES THAT PROTECT

A woman without boundaries can slowly lose sight of herself. Not because of weakness or lack of awareness, but because too many seasons were spent carrying the weight of needs and expectations that were never hers to hold. She becomes reliable, resilient, always available, always accommodating, and rarely seen. Over time, she fades into the background of her own life.

Boundaries are not punishment or ultimatums. They are not walls designed to shut people out. Boundaries are sacred definitions of where your spirit ends and another begins. They protect peace, guard purpose, and preserve identity. They create structure that allows growth without depletion, love without self loss, and support without self betrayal.

For women who lived long without limits, setting them can feel threatening. Fear often whispers that boundaries will cause loss. In truth, they remove only what is misaligned. They clear what depended on your lack of protection. They make room for what truly belongs in your life.

A boundary is not rejection. It is self honoring. It tells the world you are no longer available for depletion. It tells your inner world that voice, needs, and peace matter.

Manifest Me teaches that boundaries are essential to growth. The highest version of yourself cannot emerge while energy is constantly drained. Expansion does not occur in environments that restrict development. Elevation does not happen in relationships sustained by silence. Peace cannot coexist with constant disruption.

Boundaries require courage because they challenge familiar patterns. Agreeing to avoid conflict. Over-giving to secure connection. Shrinking to maintain harmony. Accepting disrespect to avoid loneliness. Choosing boundaries means choosing self respect over comfort, identity over insecurity, and truth over tolerance.

When boundaries are honored, energy returns. Time becomes intentional. Emotional capacity expands. Clarity sharpens. Parts of yourself once buried beneath obligation begin to reappear.

Boundaries allow no without guilt, pause without apology, and disengagement without hesitation. They grant permission to walk away from what drains and toward what aligns. They teach that disappointing others is sometimes the price of remaining loyal to yourself.

A boundary is not a wall. It is a doorway into peace, healthier connection, emotional steadiness, and the next version of you.

With boundaries in place, survival based interactions lose their hold. Relationships rooted in respect, reciprocity, and maturity become the standard. Access is no longer unlimited. Over-functioning ends. Worth is no longer measured by tolerance.

Boundaries are spiritual armor. They protect healing and growth. They are not acts of aggression but acts of alignment. They are the declaration of a woman who chooses to honor herself fully.

When a woman honors herself, everything changes. The woman who does so becomes unstoppable.

—— THE POWER OF DAILY ALIGNMENT

Manifestation is not a moment. It is a rhythm, a sacred cadence, and a daily agreement to live in alignment with the purpose God placed within you. It is choosing each day to walk in the identity He formed, rather than remaining in the version you have outgrown. Manifestation is often spoken of as a dramatic shift, yet the truest expression of it is consistency. It is shaped in ordinary obedience, not extraordinary moments.

Daily alignment with God's purpose is the decision you make each morning to choose who He is calling you to be. Even when familiar patterns try to pull you backward. It is the willingness to make choices that honors healing, vision, and obedience long before results are visible. Alignment requires presence, because it calls you to show up fully to the work God is doing within you.

Some days this alignment feels strong and assured. You speak with clarity, choose with confidence, advocate for what is right, and move with conviction. You sense the confirmation of God's hand guiding your steps and feel yourself walking deeper into purpose.

Other days alignment is quiet and surrendered. It looks like resting when striving is tempting, remaining silent when fear urges explanation, choosing peace over chaos, and stepping away from noise to hear God more clearly. It is trusting that stillness is not stagnation but obedience.

Alignment with God's purpose is not about perfection. It is about faithfulness. Growth is not measured by flawless obedience, but by a heart that continually returns to God. The woman who rises is not the one who never stumbles, but the one who keeps choosing alignment with His will when she does.

As you walk in daily obedience, subtle shifts begin beneath the surface. Your spirit softens and your mind renews. Your heart settles and your nervous system learns that peace is safe, because it is rooted in God. Old patterns loosen their hold, because they are no longer being fed by unconscious choices.

Momentum builds through small, faithful decisions that honor who God created you to be. Perspective shifts. Thoughts align with truth. Choices become intentional. Words carry wisdom. Expectation rises. Receiving becomes natural.

Living aligned with God's purpose affirms that transformation is not an event but a daily walk. It is the repeated decision to show up as a woman who is grounded in faith, healed by truth, led by the Spirit, and anchored in identity. As your inner life aligns with God, your outer life begins to reflect His order. Challenges may remain, but your foundation strengthens. You are no longer led by fear or reaction, but by calling.

Daily alignment with God becomes the bridge between who you were and who He created you to be. Each obedient choice draws you closer to His design. Each act of integrity reshapes your life to reflect His purpose.

This is the power of alignment with God. It transforms you one obedient step at a time, strengthens you one faithful moment at a time, and elevates you one day at a time. And before you realize it, you are living a life that mirrors His intention, not by accident, but by divine alignment.

CHAPTER 12

Your Manifest Me Affirmations

CHAPTER 12

YOUR MANIFEST ME AFFIRMATIONS

 There comes a moment in a woman's life that feels less like a decision and more like a calling. A moment when something within her rises and says, "This ends now." She refuses to shrink, to silence or betray who she is for the comfort of others. She no longer accepts a life that fails to reflect the power she carries or allows her to live beneath the truth of her identity.

There comes a time when you outgrow the story that once shaped you. You recognize that the past only has power if you continue to give it access. The woman who rises makes a decision that history is not her identity, and she no longer lives beneath the shadow of who she used to be.

She releases the habit of treating wounds like a place to live. She refuses to let pain define her personality or allow former disappointment to dictate what comes next. Instead, she steps into the present with purpose and looks ahead with confidence.

Your history may provide context, but it does not determine who you are. Elevation begins the moment you stop allowing it to lead your life.

That moment, when continuing as an outdated version of yourself is no longer acceptable, is your Manifest Me activation.

Your activation is not loud. It does not always require a dramatic shift or a grand declaration. At times it arrives quietly, like a whisper that strengthens with each passing day. It can show up as a deep awareness that the life you have been living can no longer hold the woman you are growing into. It comes with the understanding that discomfort is not failure but expansion, frustration is not punishment but misalignment, and yearning is not impatience but destiny drawing you forward.

Your Manifest Me activation is a divine interruption that prevents you from returning to old patterns and redirects you toward the life that has been waiting for you to rise.

It is the point where you stop arguing for limitation, defending doubt, or offering excuses for unreadiness. It is when you release the habit of repeating trauma more loudly than transformation.

Activation happens when you choose yourself fully, boldly, and with intention. You decide your voice will no longer be overlooked. You establish boundaries without compromise. You honor healing as essential. You recognize that identity carries more power than insecurity.

Your next level does not demand becoming someone new. It calls for uncovering who has always been there, hidden beneath fear, responsibility, disappointment, or survival. It invites you to step deeper into truth, to rise into the self life tried to silence, and to embody the woman who has always lived within you.

Activation is not perfection. It is permission. Permission to rise, evolve, desire more, and walk in fullness without apology.

Your Manifest Me activation is the remembrance of who you are. It is the moment clarity returns and power comes back into view. When your spirit awakens and quietly affirms, this is who you were always meant to be.

It is the moment you reclaim your identity from the grip of old wounds. You begin to understand that every blessing you have prayed for is already tied to the version of you that is rising. The love you seek, the peace you long for, the abundance meant for you, and the opportunities you envision all align with an elevated sense of self rather than a wounded one.

Once activation occurs, life starts to shift. Not because something magical appears, but because you do. Your presence changes. Your voice carries clarity. Your choices become intentional. Your thoughts expand. Your expectations rise, and your ability to receive deepens.

Activation is the step onto the path your future self has been calling you toward. It is the decision to no longer let an old story define a new identity. It is a commitment to alignment over attachment, purpose over comfort, truth over fear, and growth over excuses. This is your permission to your return to yourself.

When a woman embraces her becoming, there is no return to what she has outgrown. She moves forward with confidence and conviction into the life that has been waiting for her to recognize her power.

— I AM THE WOMAN WHO RECEIVES

I awaken to a new truth about myself.
I stop shrinking into the familiar and begin stepping boldly into the fullness of who I am.
I open my hands, my heart, and my life to everything aligned with my becoming.

I activate the identity of a woman who receives.
I am rising into a version of myself who welcomes the very things I once ran from.

I receive love that is consistent.
I receive support that is reliable.
I receive peace that stays.
I receive abundance that flows freely into my life.

I choose to step into a posture of receiving because my spirit is done rehearsing.
struggle.
I am done fighting for what is already mine.
I am done believing blessings must be earned through exhaustion.
I am done mistaking survival for identity.

This activation marks the moment I choose ease over chaos, alignment over effort, and worthiness over insecurity.

I declare these truths over myself:
I am worthy of receiving.
I am safe to receive.
I am open to receiving.
I am aligned to receive.
I am ready to receive it.

I activate the unblocked, unrestricted, unburdened version of myself.
I activate the version who trusts that what is meant for me will never require self-betrayal to maintain.

I now invite love without bracing for loss.
I now accept support without apologizing.
I now welcome abundance without shrinking.
I now receive opportunities without sabotaging.
I now embrace goodness without questioning if I deserve it.

I am the woman who receives.
And from this moment forward, my life rises to match this truth.

— I AM THE WOMAN WHO TRUSTS HERSELF

I return to my own voice.

I reclaim the power I once scattered in the opinions, reactions, and expectations of others.

I decide that my intuition, my wisdom, and my inner knowing are no longer up for debate.

I activate the identity of a woman who trusts herself.

I trust my voice.

I trust my decisions.

I trust my discernment.

I trust my intuition.

I trust my ability to navigate anything that comes my way.

I am no longer easily swayed by outside noise.

I am no longer confused by mixed messages.

I am no longer seeking validation from places that were never meant to confirm me.

The answers I once searched for everywhere else, I now find within myself.

I am grounded.

I am clear.

I am steady.

I am my own safe place.

My emotions no longer override my wisdom.

My fear no longer silences my intuition.

My past no longer clouds my present guidance.

I honor my inner voice even when it whispers.

I honor my instincts even when they challenge my comfort.

I honor my truth even when others do not understand it.

I can handle what life brings because I no longer abandon myself in difficult moments.
I can make aligned decisions because I am no longer ruled by insecurity.
I can protect my own heart because I know my worth deeply and unapologetically.

Manifest Me has taught me that the wounds that once made me doubt myself are no longer in control.
I am healing.
I am rising.
I am remembering.

Self-trust is not something I hope for. It is something I embody.
Every day, I grow stronger in my knowledge.
Every day, I become more confident in my choices.
Every day, I anchor myself deeper into the truth of who I am.

I am the woman who trusts herself.
And because I trust myself, I am unstoppable.

—— I AM THE WOMAN WHO CHOOSES HER FUTURE

I activate the identity of a woman who chooses her future.
I am done living from old stories.
I am done making decisions rooted in survival.
I am done letting my past dictate my next chapter.
I am done responding to life from wounds that no longer define me.

I choose my future by choosing myself.
I choose my future by choosing my purpose.
I choose my future by choosing alignment over attachment.
I choose my future by becoming the woman my destiny requires.

I release the version of myself that I learned to settle.
I release the habits that kept me stagnant.
I release the relationships that kept me small.
I release the beliefs that restricted my becoming.

I now make decisions from identity, not insecurity.
I now live from intention, not fear.
I now move from clarity, not confusion.
I now act from purpose, not from pain.

I align my habits with where I am going.
I align my energy with what I desire.
I align my choices with the woman I am becoming.
I align my environment with my highest self.

I surround myself with people who nourish my growth.
I invest in spaces that honor my evolution.
I create emotional safety for my next level.
I protect the future I am building with boundaries, vision, and self-respect.

Every step I take now is a step toward my future.
Every decision I make now reflects my worth.
Every moment I choose alignment expands my destiny.

I choose my future because I believe in my future.
I choose my future because I am worthy of the life calling my name.
I choose my future because my next level is already aligned with me, waiting for my yes.

I am the woman who chooses her future.
And with this choice, my next level begins.

— I AM THE WOMAN WHO EMBODIES WHOLENESS

This is the moment I return to myself fully, freely, unapologetically.
The moment I recognize that wholeness is not perfection but harmony.
The moment I embrace every part of who I am and honor the truth of my becoming.

I activate the identity of a woman who embodies wholeness.
I accept myself completely, the healed parts, the wounded parts, the growing parts, and the powerful parts.
I release the belief that I must be flawless to be worthy.
I release the pressure to pretend, perform, or present a version of myself that denies my truth.
I embrace the fullness of who I am with love and compassion.

I am no longer afraid of my wounds, I tend to them with care.
I no longer fear my emotions, I understand them, honor them, and listen to their wisdom.
I no longer hide my truth, I speak it with clarity and confidence.
I no longer run from myself, I return to myself again and again.

I honor my heart.
I honor my growth.
I honor my healing.
I honor my evolution.

I choose to live from a place of wholeness.
Wholeness in my identity.
Wholeness in my decisions.
Wholeness in my relationships.
Wholeness in my boundaries.
Wholeness in my self-respect.
Wholeness is my foundation.
Wholeness is my standard.
Wholeness is my power.

As I embody wholeness, my life aligns with my truth.
My relationships shift to reflect my self-respect.
My opportunities expand to match my identity.
My environment adjusts to the energy I now hold.
Everything connected to me rises because I am rising in wholeness.

Manifest Me has taught me that the more whole I become, the more aligned my life becomes.
I am no longer fragmented internally.
I am no longer divided within myself.
I am no longer living from pieces. I am living from my power.

Every part of me is welcome.
Every part of me is honored.
Every part of me is integrated.

I am the woman who embodies wholeness.
And because I am whole, I am powerful.
Because I am whole, I am aligned.
Because I am whole, I am unstoppable.

— I AM THE WOMAN WHO HEALS WITHOUT WAITING FOR APOLOGIES

I release myself from emotional captivity.
The moment I decide that my healing will not be postponed, delayed, or held hostage by someone else's silence.
The moment I reclaim my power from every person who was unwilling or unable to acknowledge their impact.

I activate the identity of a woman who heals without waiting for apologies.
I am no longer waiting for someone to validate the pain I felt, I validate myself.
I am no longer waiting for someone to understand what they did, I understand what it taught me.
I am no longer waiting for closure, I am creating my own.
I am no longer waiting for someone to take responsibility, I am taking responsibility for my healing.

I choose to rise without permission.
I choose to release without reconciliation.
I choose to move forward without a confession.
I choose to free myself from the emotional debts others refuse to pay.

My healing does not depend on their maturity.
My wholeness does not require their apology.
My future does not hinge on their acknowledgment.
My peace does not wait for their participation.

I am healing because I deserve healing, not because they deserve forgiveness.
I am releasing the wound because I am done reliving it.
I am letting go because holding on has nothing left to offer me.
I am choosing myself because they were never capable of choosing me in the way I needed.

I no longer replay the injury, I rewrite my identity.
I no longer fixate on what was lost, I focus on what is rising within me.
I no longer expect someone else to acknowledge my worth, I walk in my worth unapologetically.

I reclaim the parts of me I abandoned while waiting for someone else to make things right.
I reclaim my voice.
I reclaim my power.
I reclaim my peace.
I reclaim my future.

My healing is my choice.
My freedom is my birthright.
My rise is inevitable.

By choosing to heal without waiting, I break every chain that once tied me to people, places, or memories that could not honor me.
I free myself emotionally, spiritually, and mentally.
I become the woman even heartbreak could not destroy.

I am the woman who heals without waiting for apologies.
And because I heal, I rise fully, powerfully, and without hesitation.

This is the moment I release myself from the guilt I have silently carried.
The moment I stop punishing myself for the choices I made when I was simply trying to survive.
The moment I choose compassion over condemnation and grace over guilt.

——I AM THE WOMAN WHO FORGIVES HERSELF

I activate the identity of a woman who forgives herself.
I forgive myself for staying too long in places that did not honor me.
I forgive myself for ignoring the red flags I was not emotionally ready to confront.
I forgive myself for abandoning my needs while trying to hold everyone else together.
I forgive myself for shrinking to keep the peace, even when it cost me my voice.
I forgive myself for the mistakes I made while navigating pain, confusion, and heartbreak.

I release the version of me who did not know what I know now.
She was not foolish, she was learning.
She was not weak, she was surviving.
She was not clueless, she was doing her best with the emotional tools she had.
She was not the problem, she was the beginning of my evolution.

I honor her for getting me to this moment.
I thank her for enduring what she should not have had to carry.
I acknowledge her strength, her resilience, her effort, her hope.
But I no longer shame her. I free her.

Self-forgiveness is my doorway to freedom.
I release the emotional weight that has been sitting on my chest.
I break the chains of shame that have kept me small.
I detach from the guilt that tried to overshadow my growth.

I choose to see my journey not as a story of mistakes, but as a story of becoming.
Every misstep taught me.
Every heartbreak shaped me.
Every lesson strengthened me.
Every chapter prepared me.

I no longer carry blame for who I was. I carry gratitude for who I am becoming.
The woman I am becoming cannot thrive under the weight of the woman I used to be.
So I lay that weight down now, fully, completely, unapologetically.

I step forward in compassion.
I step forward in clarity.
I step forward in wholeness.
I step forward in love for myself.

I am the woman who forgives herself.
And because I forgive myself, I rise free, healed, and ready for my next level.

—— I AM THE WOMAN WHO IS NO LONGER AVAILABLE FOR CHAOS

This is the moment I release my attachment to anything that disrupts my spirit.
The moment I decide that my peace is priceless.
The moment I choose alignment as my standard and refuse to negotiate with disorder, dysfunction, or emotional instability.

I activate the identity of a woman who is no longer available for chaos.
I am no longer entertained by what drains me.
I am no longer attracted to what wounds me.
I am no longer tolerant of what confuses me.
I am no longer accessible to people or situations that thrive on instability.

Manifest Me has transformed my spirit so deeply that chaos no longer appeals to me.
Peace is my new requirement.
Consistency is my new standard.
Emotional safety is my new baseline.
Stability is my new language.
Alignment is my new expectation.

I choose environments that nourish me.
I choose relationships that ground me.
I choose conversations that elevate me.
I choose experiences that honor me.

What once felt normal now feels disruptive.
What once felt exciting now feels exhausting.
What once felt familiar now feels misaligned.
Chaos is no longer my comfort zone. It is my warning sign.

I instantly notice when someone is inconsistent with me.
I immediately recognize when someone's intentions do not match their behavior.
I feel the shift in my spirit when someone's instability tries to spill into my life.
And instead of trying to fix it, tolerate it, or earn better treatment, I walk away.

I refuse to confuse chaos with passion.
I refuse to confuse confusion with chemistry.
I refuse to confuse instability with love.
I refuse to allow emotional turbulence to masquerade as connection.

I am the woman who protects her peace with boundaries, self-respect, and discernment.
I am the woman who walks away from confusion without hesitation.
I am the woman who rejects instability and embraces emotional maturity.
I am the woman who refuses to participate in dysfunction at any cost.

I am the woman who is no longer available for chaos.
And because I am no longer available for chaos, I am fully available for peace, purpose, and alignment.

— I AM THE WOMAN WHO EMBRACES A NEW LEVEL OF PEACE

I am stepping into a peace that transforms me from the inside out.
This peace is not the absence of challenges, it is the presence of grounding.
It is the calm that rises within me no matter what happens around me.
It is the certainty that I am rooted, centered, and aligned with who I am becoming.

I activate the identity of a woman who fully embraces a new level of peace.
I honor the quiet voice inside me that knows when something is not aligned.
I listen to the guidance in my spirit that protects my wellbeing.
I guard my peace as if it were sacred, because it is.
I protect my energy with intention, wisdom, and grace.

I choose conversations that nourish me.
I choose environments that strengthen me.
I choose connections that honor my growth.
I choose rhythm over rush, clarity over confusion, presence over pressure.

Peace is no longer something I hope for.
Peace is who I am.
Peace is my posture.
Peace is my standard.
Peace is my daily intention.
Peace is the atmosphere I create everywhere I go.

I am no longer available for anything that disturbs my spirit.
I release situations that drain me.
I detach from relationships that destabilize me.
I remove myself from environments that disrupt my grounding.
My peace is too valuable to be negotiated.

Because I have created peace within myself, I am now a magnet for people, opportunities, and relationships that honor that peace.
Life begins to mirror the calm I hold inside.
Doors open that align with my serenity.
Love flows that respects my boundaries.
Opportunities appear that reflect my inner stability.

I am the woman who moves with softness, strength, and spiritual certainty.
I am the woman who is grounded, centered, and aligned.
I am the woman who embraces peace so deeply that anything chaotic cannot stay.
I am the woman who protects her inner world with unwavering devotion.
I am the woman who embraces a new level of peace, and I rise from that peace daily.

— I AM THE WOMAN WHO WALKS IN HER POWER

I am stepping fully into the power that has always belonged to me.
My power is not defined by titles, accomplishments, or applause.
My power lives within me, in my presence, my clarity, my identity, and my self-trust.
I am grounded in who I am, and I no longer dim or hide the parts of me that were designed to shine.

I am the woman who embodies her power unapologetically.
I am the woman who honors her gifts boldly.
I am the woman who trusts her identity deeply.
I am the woman who walks in her power daily, intentionally, and without hesitation.

I am powerful.
I am aligned.
I am rising, and I walk in my power with grace, courage, and certainty.

I activate the truth that my power is internal, unshakable, and undeniable.
I walk into every room with confidence because I know I belong wherever my purpose leads me.
I move with intention because I no longer operate from fear or insecurity.
I speak with clarity because my voice matters.
I lead with conviction because I trust my own wisdom.

I no longer shrink myself for anyone.
I no longer apologize for my brilliance.
I no longer minimize my gifts to make others feel comfortable.
I no longer carry people who refuse to rise with me.

I release the habit of negotiating with instability.
I let go of relationships that drain me.
I refuse to participate in environments that dishonor my worth.
I stand in my truth even when others are intimidated by my light.

I understand now that my power is not arrogance. My power is alignment.
It is my reminder to the world, and to myself, that I was created to rise.

As I walk in my power, I open the door for other women to rise too.
My strength becomes a permission slip for others to embrace their own.
My confidence becomes a reflection of what is possible.
My authenticity becomes an invitation for others to be free.

—— I AM THE WOMAN WHO LOVES WITHOUT LOSING HERSELF

I am stepping into a love that honors who I am, not a love that requires me to abandon myself.
I no longer believe that love demands my silence, my shrinking, or my self-sacrifice.
I release the old narratives that taught me I had to disappear in order to be loved.
Today, I choose a new truth: I can love deeply without losing me.

I honor my voice in love.
I honor my needs in love.
I honor my boundaries in love.
I honor my identity in love.

I understand now that real love does not ask me to dim my light or suffocate my soul.
Real love embraces my fullness.
Real love welcomes my truth.
Real love amplifies my spirit instead of draining it.
And because I know this, I refuse to participate in any connection that requires me to shrink.

I give from overflow, not exhaustion.
I show up from abundance, not desperation.
I connect from emotional security, not fear.
I love with intention, not instability.

I am learning to love in a way that includes me, not erases me.
I am choosing relationships where my presence is valued, my emotions are respected, and my truth is safe.
I am choosing environments where I do not have to choose between love and self-respect, where I can honor both at the same time.
I am choosing connections that allow me to be seen, held, chosen, and understood without compromising the woman I am becoming.

I love without losing myself because I refuse to abandon the woman I fought so hard to rediscover.
I love without losing myself because my identity is sacred.
I love without losing myself because peace is my priority.
I love without losing myself because I am whole.
I love without losing myself because I am aligned.
I love without losing myself because I am worthy of a love that feels like freedom, not captivity.

I am the woman who loves boldly and authentically,
and I am the woman who remains fully herself while doing so.

— I AM THE WOMAN WHO KNOWS SHE IS THE PRIZE

I am stepping into the truth of my worth.
Not loudly, not boastfully, but with a quiet confidence that rises from within me.
I no longer question whether I am enough. I know I am a woman of value, depth, and intention.
I know that my presence is a gift, my heart is a privilege, and my energy is not easily replaced.

I am the prize.
I no longer audition for anyone's affection.
I no longer perform to earn love.
I no longer beg for effort, attention, or consideration.
I refuse to shrink myself for approval or lose myself for validation.

I carry myself with the serene confidence of a woman who understands her worth without needing to prove it.
I honor myself.
I respect myself.
I choose myself.
And because I do, I expect the same from anyone who enters my life.

I know now that recognizing my worth is not arrogance. It is alignment.
It is sacred self-regard.
It is the understanding that I am whole, powerful, and deeply deserving of intentional love and genuine connection.
If someone cannot see my value, I no longer internalize it as a lack within me.
I no longer reinterpret their inability to appreciate me as a reflection of my inadequacy.
Their lack of recognition is not my burden. It is their limitation.

I release the need to convince anyone of my worth.
I release the desire to be chosen by those who cannot honor me.
I release every pattern, connection, and mindset that caused me to forget the truth of who I am.

I remember: I am irreplaceable.
I am unforgettable.
I am a blessing.
I am the prize.

And I move through the world with the confidence, grace, and certainty of a woman who finally recognizes the sacred value she carries.

CONCLUSION

The Manifested You

CONCLUSION

THE MANIFESTED YOU

 There is a moment in every woman's life when she finally realizes that she can no longer live at the level of who she used to be. Not because she failed, but because she has outgrown the version of herself that was shaped by survival. She senses that something within her is awakening. Something ancient, powerful, and true. This is the moment of your becoming.

The journey you've taken through these pages was never about creating a new identity. It was about reclaiming the one that life tried to make you forget. It was about returning to the woman underneath the disappointments, the responsibilities, the heartbreak, the expectations, and the silence. You faced the truths that once made you shrink. You revisited the parts of your story you tried to outrun. You questioned the beliefs that kept you small. You seen your patterns with clarity instead of shame. And you have begun healing in places you once refused to touch.

You have done the brave work, the inner work, the emotional work, the identity work, and the work that women often avoid. Because it required honesty, courage, and disruption. And through that work, the fog has lifted. You can see yourself now. Not the version of you who was shaped by old wounds and old patterns, but the woman you were always meant to become. The woman who stands tall in her truth, and protects her peace. A woman who no longer apologizes for her voice, entertains misalignment, or minimizes her brilliance. But a woman who has returned home to herself.

The woman you are today is not the woman who began this book. You have softened in the right places and strengthened in the necessary ones. You have expanded your awareness and sharpened your boundaries. You have learned to receive, release, rise, and to return to yourself again and again. And this is just the beginning.

You will continue to evolve as you honor yourself more deeply. Grow as you follow your intuition with confidence. You will advance to elevate as you choose alignment over attachment. You will prevail and thrive as you make decisions from identity and not insecurity. The life you desire is not waiting on a miracle. It is waiting on your consistency, your courage, your intention, and your willingness to remain aligned with the woman you are becoming.

So walk forward knowing this: You are worthy of every good thing you imagine. Capable of building the life your soul longs for. Powerful beyond measure. You are whole, even on the days you feel undone. Enough, even when the world tries to convince you otherwise. And you are allowed, fully allowed, to choose yourself without guilt, fear, or hesitation.

This is your season of rising, your season of clarity and expansion. This is your Manifest Me season. And as you step into the next chapter of your life, may you do so boldly, gracefully, unapologetically, and with the full understanding that the world has not yet seen the best version of you. But she's here now. **And she is ready.**

Manifest ME Declarations

MANIFEST ME DECLARATIONS

I declare that from this day forward
I will no longer shrink to make others comfortable.
I will no longer negotiate my worth,
silence my voice,
or betray myself to maintain connections that were never meant to carry me into my next level.

I declare that I am choosing myself
with boldness,
with intention,
with conviction.
I choose my peace because it is sacred.
I choose my healing because it is necessary.
I choose my growth because it aligns with my destiny.
I choose my identity because it is the foundation of everything I desire.

I declare that I am worthy
of love that is steady, stable, and safe,
of opportunities that honor my gifts,
of relationships that see me, value me, and support me,
of abundance that reflects my divine identity.

I declare that I no longer fear the woman I am becoming.
I embrace her.
I honor her.
I rise with her.
I walk with her.
I allow her to guide me into the life that has been waiting for me.

I declare that I am stepping into my Manifest Me season
the season where I trust myself completely,
where I command my life boldly,
where I receive without resistance,
where I move with grace and power,
where I embody the fullness of my calling.

This is my becoming.
This is my shift.
This is my rise.
This is my identity.
This is my Manifest Me era.

I walk into it with confidence,
with courage,
with clarity,
fully awake,
fully aligned,
fully unstoppable.

Encouragement

ENCOURAGEMENT

 As you close this book, pause to acknowledge yourself. Recognize the woman who pressed forward despite exhaustion. Acknowledge the one who endured seasons she feared would undo her. See the strength of the woman who carried heavy responsibilities quietly, healed unseen wounds, and rose from moments meant to defeat her.

You are extraordinary, not because of flawlessness, but because you continued to show up for your own life. Direction felt unclear, yet you kept moving forward. Confidence wavered, but perseverance stayed. Your worth was questioned, and still something deep within you knew that quitting was never the answer.

Let this be your reminder that you are not behind, broken, late, or in lack of what you need. You are in the process of becoming, and that process requires time and grace. The place you stand now is not the end. It is the foundation of what is being formed next. Continue to trust your journey. Choose healing again and again, and stay connected to who you truly are. Honor your voice, protect your boundaries, and remain open to what lies ahead. More is possible for you, and it is already unfolding.

Your future is not dependent on perfection. It is shaped by your willingness to be fully present. Move forward through each aligned decision, trusting that readiness can exist alongside uncertainty. Strength remains within you, even when fear attempts to speak louder. Worthiness is already yours, simply because you are here.

Continue forward, rise higher and allow yourself space to evolve. The world has yet to experience the fullness of who you are, but in time, it will.

Author's Note

AUTHOR'S NOTE

 Writing this book was not just an act of creation. It was an exploit of remembrance. These words were shaped from my own journey of healing. I wrote them for the woman who feels what I have felt, walked where I have walked, questioned her worth, and battled cycles she did not know how to break. This book is for the woman who is tired of surviving and ready to live. The woman who is ready to stand in her truth without apology, and the one who knows there is more inside her. My hope is that every page reminds you of the truth you may have forgotten. Now that you've read the book, you realize you are powerful, chosen, worthy, capable, and enough. Thank you for allowing me to guide you through this transformation. I appreciate you for trusting these words, and saying yes to yourself. It is my desire that this is not the end of your journey, but the beginning of your elevation. Your Manifest Me era has begun, and I am honored to be apart of the woman you are rising into.

With love,

Teshia

My Prayer For You

MY PRAYER FOR YOU

 Heavenly Father,

I thank You for every woman who has finished reading this book. I pray that what she has read does not end on the page, but lives within her and continues to gently transform her from the inside out. Let this book remain more than words. Let it be a mirror, a guide, and a healing invitation that continues to draw her closer to who You created her to be.

Father, I ask that she continues to grow in wisdom, clarity, and character. Where there has been brokenness, bring wholeness. Shape her heart, renew her mind, and strengthen her purpose beyond this moment.

I declare, according to Your Word, that she will prosper and be in good health, even as her soul prospers. Let her body remain strengthened, her mind renewed, and her spirit nourished daily. May alignment continue in every area of her life spiritually, emotionally, physically, and financially.

Bless the work of her hands and the thoughts of her mind. Let the doors You have opened stay open, and permanently close the doors that no longer serve Your will for her life. Surround her with divine favor, wise counsel, and healthy relationships that sustain her growth.

Most of all, Lord, let her leave this book knowing she is seen, loved, and chosen. May she walk forward more anchored in truth than when she began.

In Jesus' name,
Amen.

REFERENCES & ADDITIONAL RESOURCES

 The following books and online resources are provided for general informational and educational purposes. They reflect broader conversations related to identity formation, attachment patterns, emotional healing, relational dynamics, and inner security that align with the themes explored in Manifest Me. The content of this book is original and presented through the author's personal perspective, lived experience, and spiritual understanding. Inclusion of these resources does not imply endorsement, affiliation, or direct sourcing.

Books:
Attached — Amir Levine & Rachel Heller
The Power of Attachment — Diane Poole Heller
Insecure in Love — Leslie Becker-Phelps
Adult Children of Emotionally Immature Parents — Lindsay C. Gibson
Running on Empty — Jonice Webb
Reinventing Your Life — Jeffrey E. Young & Janet S. Klosko

Online Resources:
Attachment Project — https://www.attachmentproject.com
Greater Good Science Center (University of California, Berkeley) — https://greatergood.berkeley.edu

Online resources are provided for informational purposes only and are not intended to replace professional mental health care, diagnosis, or treatment.

MORE FROM TESHIA MILTON

The "See It, Say It, Believe It, Receive It: Manifest Life Affirmation Handbook" is a transformative guide designed to help individuals unlock the power of positive thinking and manifestation. Through the practice of visualization, 365 affirmations, and belief, this handbook provides practical steps for aligning your mindset with your desires and attracting abundance into your life.

"See It. Say It. Write It. Receive It. Manifest Life Affirmation Journal" is a guided journal designed to help you harness the power of manifestation through visualization, positive affirmations, and mindful writing. This journal combines daily affirmations, guided prompts, and inspiring scriptures to help you visualize your dreams, speak them with authority, write them into reality, and open your heart to receive all that God has in store for you. Each day, you'll reflect on a scripture that reinforces your power to manifest and create a life of purpose, exuberance, and peace. Whether you're manifesting goals, abundance, or personal growth, this journal offers a transformative space to align your thoughts, words, and actions with your highest aspirations.

www.ingramcontent.com/pod-product-compliance
Lightning Source LLC
Chambersburg PA
CBHW060503030426
42337CB00015B/1722